The Potting Shed

Robert Flemyng, Leueen MacGrath, Lewis Casson, Rudolph Weiss, and Sybil Thorndike in a scene from Act Three of *The Potting Shed,* at the Bijou Theatre in New York

The
Potting Shed

A PLAY IN THREE ACTS BY

Graham Greene

New York · THE VIKING PRESS

The Potting Shed

produced by Carmen Capalbo and Stanley Chase, was first presented on Tuesday, January 29, 1957, at the Bijou Theatre, New York, directed by Carmen Capalbo and designed by William Pitkin. The cast was as follows:

DR. FREDERICK BASTON	Lewis Casson
ANNE CALLIFER	Carol Lynley
SARA CALLIFER	Leueen MacGrath
MRS. CALLIFER	Sybil Thorndike
JOHN CALLIFER	Stanley Lemin
JAMES CALLIFER	Robert Flemyng
DR. KREUZER	Rudolf Weiss
CORNER	Richard Longman
MRS. POTTER	Eda Heinemann
MISS CONNOLLY	Joan Croydon
FATHER WILLIAM CALLIFER	Frank Conroy

Scenes

Act One

Act One

Act One
SCENE ONE

*It is the living room of Wild Grove one autumn afternoon—
if one were to describe the room in terms of its owner,
H. C. Callifer, a high-minded rather pedantic room and a
little outmoded. There are a lot of books, but they look, even
from a distance, dull and heavy books. One might have taken
them for works of theology if one were unaware of H. C. Callifer's reputation. Alas! how much of the world, after a period
when Callifer was classed with Wynwood Read and* The Cosmic Fallacy *with* The Martyrdom of Man, *has become unaware of that reputation. The world has changed around this
room, this house. When Callifer first built Wild Grove, plan-
ning it with the woman he loved, those factory chimneys
which now appear in the distance through the garden window did not exist. There was a grove—perhaps there was even
a wildness in Callifer himself, but more than forty years have
passed since then. The Grove has become a grave, and in the
best bedroom upstairs H. C. Callifer is dying. Throughout
the scene that follows, till the very end, we hear at times the
footsteps of those above; conversations are interrupted while
the quality of the footsteps are, as it were, assessed.*

13

The Potting Shed

When the curtain rises there is only one occupant of the living room—a man twenty years junior to Callifer himself, but twenty years at this period of life have ceased to count. Dr. Frederick Baston is now well past sixty, though he was once Callifer's youngest and cleverest disciple. His reputation grew with Callifer's, but he was never a rival. If Callifer had died at sixty, Baston would have written his biography and carried on his work, but when the tide of the world's favour receded from Callifer, it receded from Baston too. They are part of the same beach. Will any publisher now be sufficiently interested to commission a biography?

A small, tired, fussy figure, worrying too much about details, Baston is walking restlessly from one end of the living room to the other, from the fireplace with Dutch tiles to the mirror over the sofa. He carries two or three sheets of notepaper in his hand and he is learning something by heart. As he reaches the fireplace he tries out a passage, letting his hand fall.

BASTON: It needed courage in those days to meet the challenge of the churches with a—with a—(*he consults his pages again and walks back towards the mirror, reading the words in an inaudible mutter. When he reaches the mirror he shoots out another phrase*)—against the vested interests of superstition. (*He catches sight of himself in the mirror and, leaning forward, examines a sty on the lower lid of his left eye. He gives it a tentative squeeze, and then starts out on his walk again.*) Callifer's greatest book was of course *The Cosmic Fallacy*, but those who were closest to him knew what store he set by that charming pathetic study of Jesus Christ, the Palestinian religious leader, *He Was a Man.* He was a man. We can say that too, in a different sense, of Callifer. Those of us who loved him most, his wife, his sons—(*he consults his pages*) his son, his oldest friend and disciple, repeat with sorrow, "He was a man." We would be unworthy of him—(*he reaches the mirror and again against his will his finger goes up and tries the sty; a pause; he turns to pace again; a girl of thirteen comes through the garden window, unnoticed, and watches him*) unworthy of him if, if—(*he consults his pages, looks around, picks up an ash-tray from a table*) we did not recognize that these ashes that at his request I now resign to the river and the fields and the earth he loved (*he makes a motion with his ash-tray*) are all that remains. (*Back again, while the girl observes him.*) Now that the immense spaces of the empty universe, of uninhabited planets and cooling stellar systems have taken the place of the Christian God, we have Callifer to thank for a human life worthy of courageous Man. To the Christian superstition of eternal life, he bravely countered with the truth, Eternal Death.

The girl interrupts, interested, matter-of-fact.

ANNE: Has Grandfather died, Dr. Baston?

BASTON (*put out*): I'm sorry—didn't hear. . . . Where did you come from?

ANNE: The garden.

BASTON: Playing?

ANNE: Would you mind being very careful what questions you ask me?

BASTON: Why?

ANNE: There you go again. You see, I've made a vow that for one month I'll speak the exact truth—a lunar month, not a calendar. There are still eighteen days to go.

BASTON: What happens afterwards?

ANNE: I shall tell lies again like everybody else. Is Grandfather dead yet?

BASTON: He's making a wonderful fight.

ANNE: So would you, wouldn't you? It can't be very nice, being dead. Is Granny with him?

BASTON: Yes. And your father. And the doctor, of course.

ANNE: Will he last the night, do you think?

BASTON: So *you* ask questions too.

ANNE: Only when I really want to know the answer. Practical questions. That was another vow of mine. Only I'm keeping that vow forever.

BASTON: Who did you vow to?

ANNE: To the inevitability of evolution and the sacredness of man.

BASTON: It sounds a big vow.

ANNE: I got it from an essay of grandfather's, "The Credo of an Atheist." You know, I liked what you said just now about uninhabited planets.

BASTON: I can see you're a real Callifer.

ANNE: Sometimes I wish this planet was uninhabited too—no human beings, only hills and rivers and sky.

BASTON: I rather like human beings.

ANNE: I don't. They are so untidy. Stomach aches, colds in the head, spots—(BASTON *automatically puts up his hand to his sty*.) Aunt Sara's in the garden, snivelling in a deck chair.

BASTON: What a hard child you are.

ANNE: It's no good being mushy, is it? It's the truth that matters. And she *is* snivelling.

BASTON: You could have said "crying."

ANNE: But crying's quite a different thing.

BASTON: I expect she's very fond of your grandfather.

ANNE: Perhaps. Or she may be snivelling for lost love, though it's not likely after all these years. I call her Aunt Sara, but strictly speaking I shouldn't, should I, not after she divorced Uncle?

BASTON (*ironically*): A courtesy title.

ANNE: I don't understand why she comes here, and not Uncle James.

BASTON (*uneasily*): I suppose he was too busy to come. Or perhaps his paper couldn't spare him. And it's a long way from Nottingham.

ANNE: My school is further than Nottingham. They fetched *me*.

BASTON: I expect there was some reason.

17

The Potting Shed

ANNE: They never told him Grandfather was dying.

BASTON: Nonsense.

ANNE: But I *know*. They gave me the telegrams to take to the post office. There was one to you and one to Father, even one to her. but not to him. Is he a criminal? That's a practical question.

BASTON: Of course he isn't.

ANNE: Or wicked?

BASTON: No, no.

ANNE: Or mad?

BASTON: Of course not.

ANNE: (*after a pause for thought*): Then I was quite right to do what I did.

BASTON: What did you do?

ANNE: I sent him a telegram myself.

BASTON (*in a shocked voice*): That was very, very wrong of you.

ANNE: Why?

BASTON: To upset everybody at a time like this. With your grandfather dying upstairs.

ANNE: Is Uncle a hunchback? Has he got a face of horror?

BASTON: You're a silly interfering little girl. I only hope he has the sense not to come. I shall have to warn your grand-mother.

ANNE (*pondering the word*): Warn—?

BASTON: He's not wanted here. Nobody wants him here.

ANNE (*going thoughtfully to the window*): I see. I'm sorry. (*She goes thoughtfully out through the french windows, passing Sara as she does so.*)

Sara is a woman of about thirty-six, good-looking, but carrying with her a sense of disappointment and drift.

BASTON (*holding out his sheaf of papers*): She's made me forget every word. (*He lays the papers on a table.*)

SARA: Is he dead?

BASTON: No. They'll call us at the end. Do you know what that child has done? She's sent for James.

SARA: Poor James. But is that so awful? He's got the right, hasn't he?

BASTON: And that old man has the right to die in peace.

SARA: Sometimes the dying want to forgive . . .

BASTON (*evasively*): Oh, I don't think there's anything to forgive.

SARA: It will be strange seeing James after all these years. What does a man become when a wife leaves him on his own? He ate salt on his bread and he used to take tea, not coffee, for breakfast. Those are the things one remembers. (*A pause.*) Why did they always hate him so? I don't.

19

BASTON (*hedging*): It's not hate. They never got along, that's all. Even when he was a boy . . .

SARA: I would have loved a child of mine whatever he did. (*A pause.*) Do you know, they only got fond of me after the divorce? They wrote to me so kindly then. But as long as James and I were together I was infectious. A mother generally defends her son, doesn't she?—but when I left him, I won his mother's approval.

BASTON: I shan't tell Mrs. Callifer yet. Perhaps he'll have the sense to keep away. For your sake, too, it would be painful.

SARA: Would it? I suppose so. It's very bitter when a man leaves you for nothing. I wouldn't have minded so much if he'd been in love with another woman. I could bear being beaten by someone younger, someone lovely. But I was beaten by a bed-sitting-room in Nottingham. That's all he left me for.

BASTON: I remember your house at Richmond. It was very beautiful.

SARA: But he wouldn't live in it. (*Bitterly*): It contained *me*.

BASTON: I never understood it. He always seemed so fond of you.

SARA: Do you know what it's like being married to a sleepwalker?

BASTON: I don't know anything about marriage. I never had the nerve to commit it.

The door opens and Mrs. Callifer enters—a handsome up-right figure in spite of her seventy years.

BASTON: How is he?

MRS. CALLIFER: He's sleeping again. He was conscious for nearly five minutes. I almost hoped.

BASTON: You ought to rest, Mary. Let Sara or me—

MRS. CALLIFER: I'll rest when it's over.

BASTON: You're killing yourself.

MRS. CALLIFER: Oh, no, Fred, don't worry. That would be too good. (*A pause.*) Next week we would have had our golden wedding. (*She goes over to a table where Baston has laid down his papers. Before he can interfere she has picked one up. He waits with a look of embarrassed shame.*) It reads very well, Fred. "Cooling stellar systems."

BASTON: Those are *his* words.

MRS. CALLIFER: We had a royalty statement last week. They only send them once a year now. They'd sold three copies of *The Cosmic Fallacy* for export.

BASTON: Anyway it's in print still.

MRS. CALLIFER: Oh, yes. At that rate it will be in print longer than we shall be. Christianity is the fashion now.

BASTON: A passing fashion.

MRS. CALLIFER: Of course. But how he hated those sentimental myths, virgin births, crucified Gods. (*She is thinking of something else and talks to distract herself.*) Just now,

21

from Henry's room, I thought I heard a dog barking. Did you?

BASTON: No. Perhaps a stray—

MRS. CALLIFER: I must remember to look at the wire netting on the gate. We had a lot of trouble once with dogs, messing up the flower beds.

SARA (*with a smile*): I have one now, but I never bring it.

MRS. CALLIFER: You think I'm very fussy, but you know it's not old age. I've always detested dogs, haven't I, Fred?

BASTON: Always.

MRS. CALLIFER: Parodies of men and women. I hate parodies. We both always hated parodies. Where's John?

BASTON: I thought he was with you.

SARA: He went to the post office.

MRS. CALLIFER: I hope he won't be long. (*She tries to talk very detachedly and sensibly, but she can't prevent her restless movements and the quick changes of subject that show her mind is elsewhere.*) It was good of you to do the flowers, Sara. Very nicely, too. Perhaps a little modern. I'm surprised *The Times* hasn't rung up.

SARA (*comfortingly*): The *Rationalist Review* was on the telephone an hour ago. A Mr. Minster. He was very concerned.

MRS. CALLIFER (*dismissing the comfort*): We never thought very highly of Mr. Minster. Where is Anne?

SARA: In the garden.

MRS. CALLIFER: If he becomes conscious it will be the last time. I do want him to see all the faces he loved. You, Fred, especially. (*But this statement is too near the emotion she is trying to suppress. She veers away, picking up Baston's papers.*) It was good of you to come at once, take all this trouble. You know I tried to persuade him to alter his will—about the ceremony. The River Wandle is not how he remembers it. Too much pollution from the dye factory, and the housing development has ruined the fields.

BASTON: John and I found a spot where you can only just see the chimneys—

MRS. CALLIFER: Well, of course it doesn't matter, does it? It's just a gesture, scattering ashes. People are so sentimental sometimes—about death—wishing to be buried together. (*Her voice breaks and she makes for a flower vase and begins to rearrange it.*)

SARA (*breaking the silence*): I really believe I did hear a dog.

MRS. CALLIFER: I thought I'd have Mrs. Bentham in to make new slipcovers. These are really too old. (*She desperately slides across the surface of the unfamiliar new life of a widow.*) Do you really have to go next week, Sara?

SARA: Oh, I could always make an excuse.

MRS. CALLIFER: I thought if you could stay a few more days—we might hire a car and go to the autumn flower show at Weston. I missed it last year when Henry was ill.

SARA: Of course I'll stay.

Anne comes quietly and rather secretively in through the window. She slides to a chair and takes the first book to hand.

MRS. CALLIFER: I do wish John would come back. I'd better get some patterns to show Mrs. Bentham.

SARA: I'll write for you.

MRS. CALLIFER: Why, Anne, I didn't see you come in. Where have you been?

ANNE (*carefully*): In the garden.

BASTON (*trying to be breezy*): Playing?

ANNE (*giving him a withering look—questions again*): No.

SARA: Anne, that's not the way to speak to Dr. Baston. He only wanted to know what you were doing.

Anne scowls into her book.

MRS. CALLIFER: You haven't been picking flowers again, dear, have you?

ANNE: No, Granny. (*She takes the book and tries to escape, but something in her manner attracts attention.*)

MRS. CALLIFER: Where have you been, dear?

ANNE: It's not fair, all of you asking questions. I told you my vow. You oughtn't to ask any questions till the vow's over.

MRS. CALLIFER: All the same, I *am* asking, Anne.

ANNE (*sullenly*): I've been to the potting shed.

A pause.

Mrs. Callifer: Oh. (*A pause.*) Why the potting shed? You know I don't like you going there. The gardener's complained of you knocking over the seedlings.

Anne: I didn't touch them.

Sara: What were you doing?

Anne: Oh, if you've got to know, I was shutting up a secret dog.

Baston: A secret dog?

Sara: Then we did hear a bark.

Mrs. Callifer: Do you mean a stray dog?

Anne: No. A secret dog.

Mrs. Callifer: But you know I won't have dogs here. Who does it belong to?

Anne: A man.

Sara: What man?

Anne: He's come to see Grandfather.

Sara: I said, what man?

Anne: Well, if you must know, your ex-husband.

Mrs. Callifer: James?

Anne: Yes.

Mrs. Callifer: Did you know about this, Sara?

Baston: Anne sent him a telegram.

MRS. CALLIFER: Where is he?

ANNE: I don't know. I told him you didn't like dogs. He'd forgotten. So he asked where he could put it, and I told him the potting shed. I said I'd show him the way, but he said I could do it for him. When I looked back, he'd gone. We'd meant to keep it a dark secret, but you would ask questions.

John, the eldest son, Anne's father, enters through the left door. He is correctly dressed. He will only, in the event, need a black tie to be prepared for the funeral.

JOHN: Mother, do you know who's here?

MRS. CALLIFER: James.

JOHN: I nearly ran into him.

MRS. CALLIFER: If he's here, well—of course—naturally—he's welcome. (*James enters through the garden window. He is five years younger than John, who must be nearly fifty; in some ways he looks the elder. Life hasn't dealt with him so well: he appears nervous and ill at ease, a stranger in his parents' house. His clothes are less new and less suitable.*) How are you, James? I'm glad you could come.

He kisses her cheek awkwardly. Then he sees Sara.

JAMES: Sara (*he makes an odd movement of apology*), I didn't mean to be a nuisance. I just thought if Father . . .

MRS. CALLIFER: Of course you're not a nuisance. We tele-graphed for you.

Anne looks up at this lie.

JAMES: Anne telegraphed for me (*nodding at Anne*).

MRS. CALLIFER: I told her to, James.

Anne, with a flurry of anger, goes back into the garden.

JAMES: I see.

MRS. CALLIFER: This is Frederick Baston, James. You remember Dr. Baston.

JAMES: It's so many years . . . (*They shake hands with constraint.*) How's Father?

MRS. CALLIFER: It will be any moment now.

JAMES: Can I see him?

MRS. CALLIFER: Better not—at present. He's unconscious.

There is a pause. He stands there as though surrounded by strangers as ill-at-ease as himself. Then Sara breaks the circle and goes to his side.

SARA: How are you, James?

JAMES: Oh, well, very well, Sara. And you?

SARA: Oh, I'm well, too.

JOHN: How's the paper, old man?

JAMES: That's well. And the bank?

JOHN: Oh—flourishing.

BASTON: How's the weather up north?

JAMES: It was raining when I left.

The Potting Shed

A pause.

MRS. CALLIFER: I must go to Henry. (*She leaves the room.*)

SARA: Well, let's sit down.

JOHN: If you don't mind, I want to have a word with Fred—about the ceremony.

John and Baston leave.

JAMES: The ceremony! What a cold word.

SARA: Dr. Baston is reading an oration. (*She points to the table.*) There it is.

JAMES: My mother didn't even let me know.

SARA: You heard what she said.

JAMES: It wasn't true. I had the true story from Anne. I was to be left out. Why? One's father's death is usually supposed to be important.

SARA: Perhaps it's not very important if you believe in nothing afterwards. Or do you? I ought to know. We were married for five years, but it's the tea you had for breakfast I remember. You liked it strong. Otherwise you said you couldn't taste it. Does your landlady make good tea?

JAMES: I suppose so. Sara, what's wrong with me? Why do they keep me away? I wasn't much of a husband to you, I know, but I wasn't bad, was I?

SARA: No. You weren't bad, James. It was just you weren't interested. You pretended very well and very kindly. Even in

28

bed you pretended. I used to think there was another woman somewhere. Someone like the tea, strong enough for you to taste. You couldn't taste me. What do you think about when you are alone?

JAMES: Think about?

SARA: I used to imagine you were thinking of someone else. But when you went away—there was nobody. How bored you must have been with me.

JAMES: No, I wasn't bored. I knew I made you unhappy. There seemed no point in going on. I wish you had married again, Sara. John's a born widower, but you . . .

SARA: I took a lover after you went. He didn't pretend. And then one night I woke and saw him sleeping beside me, content—and I remembered you with your eyes open, thinking of something else, and I didn't want him any more. I didn't love him any more.

JAMES: What's the good of talking importantly about love? It doesn't last like a book or a tune. It goes out with the breath, and we can always snuff that out, can't we? We're not worth loving.

SARA: Then nothing is.

JAMES: And I love nothing.

SARA (*bitterly*): You do indeed. In the night you'd wake loving Nothing. You went looking for Nothing everywhere. When you came in at night I could see you had been with Nothing all day. I was jealous of Nothing as though it was a woman; and now you sleep with Nothing every night. Oh hell, give me a cigarette.

JAMES: I don't smoke. (*Pause.*) Sara, what's wrong with me?

SARA: You're not alive. Sometimes I wanted to make you angry or sorry, to hurt you. But you never felt pain. Why did you marry me? (*James makes a gesture.*) I believe it was curiosity to see if you could feel. You didn't feel.

JAMES: I thought if I saw my father now, at the end, he'd tell me. Tell me what's wrong.

SARA: I thought I knew what it was.

JAMES: Yes?

SARA: When your mother heard about the telegram she was afraid.

JAMES: Afraid of what I'd do?

SARA: Afraid of what you are.

JAMES: A middle-aged newspaper man. I go to the office at four and usually get away by one in the morning. I sleep till nine—I mean, I stay in bed. I take the dog for a walk in the park and have a meal with Corner.

SARA: Corner?

JAMES: He shares my lodgings—a reporter on the *Globe*. My landlady has a penchant for tinned salmon. My dog likes it, but it often makes him sick. He's not a very good dog—parents unknown.

SARA: You shouldn't have brought him here. Your mother hates dogs.

JAMES: Yes, I know. I forgot. You see, our acquaintance has not been very continuous.

SARA: Don't be bitter. She's very unhappy now.

JAMES: I'm not bitter. I want to know, that's all. What's your earliest memory, Sara?

SARA: Driving a pony cart.

JAMES: I can remember nothing. Absolutely nothing. Until I was ill, just before they sent me away to school at fourteen. Lying in bed with a sore throat. A dim light burning, and a nurse—a very kind nurse, bringing me soup. I thought she was an angel— I'd seen a picture of one once, I suppose, in a shop.

SARA: I'd come and live with you at Nottingham if you wanted me.

JAMES: What about the house in Richmond?

SARA: I'd sell it. I only came here because I thought I'd see you. But I didn't dare to ask why you weren't here. (*A slight pause.*) You know, I love you, James.

JAMES: Sara— (*He comes behind her and puts his hands over her eyes.*) I could always talk to you better in the dark. Sara, I simply don't know what love is. What is it?

SARA: It's what I feel now.

JAMES: But if I took my hands away and we saw each other, I'd see—a want. Isn't there a love that just exists and doesn't want? My father's dying. He has nothing to hope for, any more, forever. When he looks at me, don't you think I might see—just love? No claim, no hope, no want. Whisky taken neat.

SARA: The strong taste.

JAMES: Yes. (*He takes away his hands. The noise of feet on the ceiling above.*) Listen. Perhaps he's woken up. I haven't seen him for fifteen years, Sara. (*She puts her head against him.*)

SARA: How your heart's beating!

JAMES: Perhaps he'll speak.

He moves a little towards the door. Mrs. Callifer's voice calls from the stairs: "John! Fred!" The noise of quick footsteps, and Mrs. Callifer enters.

MRS. CALLIFER: Where's Anne?

SARA: In the garden.

MRS. CALLIFER: Please fetch her quickly.

Sara goes out into the garden.

JAMES: Father?

MRS. CALLIFER: Yes.

JAMES: Can I go up?

MRS. CALLIFER: Please wait. The nurse has to let me know.

JAMES: There's not much time, is there?

Mrs. Callifer: He mustn't have a shock—now. (*Sara comes in with Anne.*) Go upstairs quickly, dear. Both of you. (*She steps aside for them and they go out.*)

James: I thought we had to wait for the nurse?

Mrs. Callifer (*slowly, bracing herself for the plain truth*): James, I don't want you to see him.

James: But why? I've come for that.

Mrs. Callifer: I didn't send the telegram.

James: I know. I'm going to see him, though.

He moves towards the open door, but Mrs. Callifer shuts it and stands with her fingers on the handle.

Mrs. Callifer: I don't want to be harsh. That's why I wanted to let you know afterwards. But he's got to die in peace.

James: Why should I destroy his peace?

Mrs. Callifer (*pleadingly*): I love him, James. I want so much to see the last of him. Promise me you won't move from here.

James: No! (*He shakes his head.*)

Mrs. Callifer: Then I stay. (*She leans wearily against the door.*)

James: Mother, if you love me—

Mrs. Callifer: I love him more.

James: Give me one reason. (*She doesn't answer, but she is crying.*) All right. You've won, Mother. I promise not to come.

As she goes through the door, the curtain begins slowly to fall on him alone, facing the door. He raises his head a little as though trying to hear the sounds overhead.

CURTAIN

Act One
SCENE TWO

Act One
SCENE TWO

Late evening, two days later.

Baston, John, and James are drinking whisky in a group round a table on which a number of manuscripts and books are piled. John is going through them. Sara and Anne sit on the other side of the room, reading, but in Anne's case the reading is an excuse for sitting up and listening.

JOHN: Look at this. Strange the things he kept—an invitation to a college dinner in 1910. (*He drops it into a wastepaper basket.*) Do you know what all these books are? Old visitors' books.

JAMES (*ironically*): Perhaps he thought the signatures might become valuable.

JOHN (*taking him seriously*): I hadn't thought of that. Wells came several times. And here is Bertrand Russell for lunch. Do you think I ought to keep them?

JAMES: No. (*He takes one at random and opens it.*) Ah, here is Dr. Baston's autograph.

BASTON: You'll find me on a lot of pages, I'm afraid.

JAMES: August third to eighth, 1919. Do you remember that visit?

BASTON: As a matter of fact, I do. The first summer after the war. It was beautiful weather. We played cricket in the Long Meadow. You children too.

JAMES: I don't remember. (*But he is trying hard.*)

BASTON: It was before they built the dye factory. You could understand then why the house was called Wild Grove. There was a wood of beech and wild-nut trees where the housing development is. I remember I hit a six into the River Wandle.

JAMES: I must have been nearly eight that summer. (*He sits with the book on his knees, thinking.*)

John discards more papers into the wastepaper basket.

SARA (*closing her book*): I think I'll go to bed. Are you coming, Anne?

ANNE: No, I want to finish the chapter.

SARA: It's long past your bedtime.

BASTON: It was so hot we all played in bathing drawers. What happy times those were!

ANNE: I won't be long, Aunt Sara.

SARA (*pauses by the men as she goes out*): I thought your oration was spoken very well, Dr. Baston.

BASTON: Thank you, my dear.

SARA: Are you really going tomorrow, James?

JAMES: Yes, I have to.

SARA: I'll see you in the morning?

JAMES: I'm leaving very early.

SARA: I'll get up. (*She touches his hair with her hand.*) Good night, dear.

JAMES: Good night, Sara. (*He stares down at the visitors' book without looking up. She goes slowly out.*)

BASTON: I thought of that game this afternoon. We were in the same field. You children called your father the demon bowler. He bowled underarm, but very fast.

JOHN: Yes, I remember. With a tennis ball!

JAMES (*after a pause*): I don't remember.

JOHN: Poor Father! Here are the expenses of a holiday in France in 1910. Bottle of red wine, one franc fifty centimes. Filed for future reference.

JAMES (*opening another of the books*): Nineteen twenty-five—that was the year I was ill, the year I went away to school. Who's William Callifer?

BASTON: Don't you even remember your own uncle?

JAMES: No. Didn't he get a telegram either—or is he dead?

Anne looks sharply up.

JOHN: Father never had much to do with him.

37

JAMES (*turning the pages*): He was here for three days that autumn.

BASTON: It was the last time. He behaved rather badly.

JOHN: It was bad enough to have a convert in the family—but when he became a priest . . .

JAMES: I'm glad I'm not the only pariah among the Callifers. (*He puts the book down.*)

JOHN: Bertrand Russell again. I hope he was worth his meal ticket.

Anne closes her book and comes over.

BASTON: How are the vows, Anne?

ANNE (*she pointedly ignores so silly a question*): Uncle James, if I put out some water in the hall, will you take it to the potting shed?

JAMES (*uneasy*): The potting shed?

ANNE: To your dog, stupid.

JAMES: Couldn't you do it for me? You've been looking after him.

ANNE: I think Spot would prefer you, after what happened this afternoon. If I go now, he'll think he's still in disgrace. Granny was so angry.

JAMES: But I don't where it is, Anne.

ANNE: You've seen me going there often enough. Down the path by the laurels. You can't miss it. Good night, Daddy. (*She kisses her father.*) Good night, Dr. Baston (*stiffly*).

BASTON: Good night, Anne. (*Sententiously*): It's a good thing when a sad day ends.

ANNE: Oh, it wasn't all sad, was it? I thought it was awfully funny when Spot came bounding along looking for Uncle James, and you dropped the ashes.

BASTON: It wasn't very nice for your grandmother. It spoiled the ceremony.

ANNE: You were just saying, "I now consign to the river . . ." You could have altered it quickly and said, "I now consign to Long Meadow."

JOHN: Do go to bed, Anne.

ANNE (*pausing at the door*): You won't forget the water, Uncle James?

He shakes his head. Anne leaves.

BASTON: How heartless children are.

JOHN: Oh, I don't think she meant it that way. She was being practical, that's all. Her mother was the same. Help yourselves to whisky.

BASTON: Thanks. It *was* unfortunate you brought that dog.

JAMES: I know. I forgot. (*They help themselves.*) Was Mother asleep when you went upstairs?

JOHN: She seemed to be.

JAMES: You'll say good-bye for me, won't you? Say I'm sorry I—butted in.

BASTON: You exaggerate.

JAMES: Do I? (*A pause while he looks at the visitors' book again.*) Fancy a Callifer being a priest.

BASTON: As a priest he hasn't been exactly a success.

JAMES: People believe, don't they, some of them, that the spirits of the dead will pass over a glass of wine, rippling the surface? (*He regards his whisky.*) Will whisky do? Can you invoke the dead with whisky?

JOHN: What nonsense you talk, James.

BASTON (*dryly*): It's the method your uncle is said to use.

JAMES: You mean he drinks?

BASTON: Inordinately.

JAMES: How unlike a Callifer. Well, I'm going to bed.

BASTON: Don't forget the dog.

JAMES: Oh, the dog. (*Something disturbs him.*) Surely he can do without water just tonight. (*He goes to the garden window and looks out at the dark.*) He's asleep. And it's late. It will do in the morning.

JOHN: So long as he doesn't wake Mother with his howling.

JAMES: Couldn't you do it, John? It's very dark outside. You know the way.

JOHN: And be bitten at the end of it? Look after your own dog, James.

JAMES: I've forgotten where the potting shed is.

JOHN: Anne told you. Down the laurel walk. You can't miss it. And there's a flashlight on the hall table.

A distant howl.

BASTON: Listen. He *is* howling.

JOHN: You'd better let him out and keep him in your room. (*Another howl.*) Oh, for God's sake, James, do something. He'll keep everybody awake. (*James goes unwillingly out to the hall. A door closes.*) He hasn't changed. Always difficult. Do you think I ought to look through all these books, Fred?

BASTON: I wouldn't bother. They wouldn't fetch much.

JOHN: We did have some distinguished visitors. How do you pronounce C-Z-E-C-H-W-Y-I-C-Z?

BASTON: Oh, that was the Polish delegation. A disappointing lot. Very unsound on evolution.

Mrs. Callifer enters. She is in her dressing-gown.

MRS. CALLIFER: I didn't mean to interrupt. . . .

JOHN: Can't you sleep, Mother?

MRS. CALLIFER: I did, for a little. Has James gone to bed?

JOHN: Yes. And we are just going. (*He drops the books into the basket.*) Try to sleep.

MRS. CALLIFER: A book will help. (*Sadly*): You've done a lot of tidying already, John. You and Fred have been very helpful. (*She goes over to the bookcase and picks almost at random.*) Well, this ought to send me to sleep. Oh, I'm sorry, it's one of yours, Fred. (*She opens it and reads the dedication.*) "To Henry Callifer, a great leader and a great friend." Strange, that doesn't sound true any longer.

BASTON: I don't follow you.

MRS. CALLIFER: How could you, Fred? But for nearly fifty years I've looked after his laundry. I've seen to his household. I've paid attention to his—allergies. He wasn't a leader. I can see that now. He was someone I protected. And now I'm unemployed. Please go to bed both of you, and leave me alone.

JOHN (*standing up*): You have your family, Mother.

MRS. CALLIFER: You don't need protection, John. You're like me, a professional protector. It wasn't what I intended to be. But men either form us with their strength, or they form us with their weakness. They never let us be.

BASTON: Mary, you mustn't—

MRS. CALLIFER: Poor James had to suffer. We did him a great wrong, Henry and I. Why shouldn't he know—as much as we know?

BASTON: It would be a mistake. After all these years. And what *do* we know?

JOHN: You've never told me anything.

MRS. CALLIFER (*ignoring him*): I don't want your empty

42

spaces, Fred. I don't want anything except Henry. Henry alive. Somehow. Somewhere.

BASTON (*with a gesture of comfort*): Mary—

MRS. CALLIFER: I've often talked so harshly of him to you, and yet I loved him.

BASTON: So did I.

MRS. CALLIFER: Please, John, both of you, go away. I'll be all right when I'm alone. But I'm not strong enough yet for sympathy.

JOHN: Come up soon, Mother.

MRS. CALLIFER: In a little while. But it's such a large room. I'll move into Sara's when she goes. Good night, my dear. (*She kisses John on the cheek.*) Good night, Fred. (*She lifts her cheek for him to kiss.*)

BASTON: You'll call me if there's anything . . .

MRS. CALLIFER: Of course. You must look after that sty, Fred. You've been picking at it again. And you a doctor.

JOHN (*leaving*): Good night, Mother.

BASTON (*absent-mindedly, at the door*): I'll look in at Henry— (*He stops, aghast at what he's said.*)

MRS. CALLIFER: Don't worry, Fred. We'll all make that mistake for a while. Today when I was ordering lunch I said, "Not string beans." He always hated them. Now we can have them every day.

43

BASTON: Mistakes like that are a kind of immortality. You remember Samuel Butler's sonnet:

> "Yet meet we shall, and part, and meet again,
>   Where dead men meet, on lips of living men."

As long as there are you and I—and his books.

MRS. CALLIFER: Yes, three copies for export. There was once a Callifer Club, do you remember?

BASTON: Yes. Mary, I was going to write to Macmillan's and suggest a biography, an intimate biography with letters. . . .

MRS. CALLIFER: Don't, Fred. Wait until a publisher writes to you. I'd rather hope than collect polite refusals.

BASTON: As you wish. But when he had his first bad illness, they did suggest . . .

MRS. CALLIFER: That was thirty years ago. Your oration will do just as well, Fred, for those who are interested. I'll have it printed. For private distribution only. Do you think two hundred copies? There may be still some members of the club. . . . It was very dear and generous of you. If only that wretched dog— Oh, well. I'll read myself to sleep with your book, Fred. Good night.

BASTON: Good night, Mary.

MRS. CALLIFER: Turn out the light, dear, as you go.

He goes out.

And Mrs. Callifer sits in a straight armchair under a reading lamp. She begins to read, but she can't concentrate, and al-

44

most at once she puts the book down. The door to the garden opens and closes, and she turns with a wild movement, as though she expected to see someone. Then, with knowledge of the truth, and with the despair of it, she whispers, "Henry . . ." The french window opens and James enters. There is a tenseness in his manner, an impression of fear, and he carries a bowl of water. He sees his mother and stands awkwardly, like a boy caught in an absurd action.

MRS. CALLIFER (*peering into the shadows*): Is that you, James?

JAMES: Yes, Mother.

MRS. CALLIFER: I thought you were in bed. What's that you've got in your hand, dear?

It's as if in this half-darkness they have both shed thirty years. A middle-aged mother is talking to her half-grown son. They have different interests, but they are gentle and kind to each other.

JAMES: A bowl of water—for the dog.

MRS. CALLIFER: Oh. (*It's too late at night to be unkind about the animal.*)

JAMES: I started to take it to him. But, Mother—

MRS. CALLIFER: Yes, dear?

JAMES: I was too frightened.

MRS. CALLIFER: Why frightened? Was it the darkness, dear?

JAMES: No. I don't mind the dark.

45

MRS. CALLIFER: Then what was it? (*He puts the bowl down and comes slowly towards her ring of lamplight.*) Tell me what happened, dear.

JAMES: I didn't want to go. I was frightened before I left the house, just as though I knew someone was waiting for me, among the laurels, on the path to the potting shed.

Mrs. Callifer makes a movement which might be one of fear or tenderness.

MRS. CALLIFER: My poor James.

He sits down, like a child, on the floor at her feet.

JAMES: Mother, I'm sorry. About the dog and coming here. Disturbing you.

She runs her hand over his head. It's almost as though the constraint between them were at last breaking down.

MRS. CALLIFER: My dear, don't worry. You're my son, James.

JAMES: Yes, I'm your son, Mother. Will you tell me, please, now—now Father's not here—what's wrong?

MRS. CALLIFER: Wrong?

JAMES: Wrong with me. So that you were afraid to see me. Oh, except between trains at Nottingham when you were taking Anne to school. Do you remember when we met that time for tea at the Kardomah? I made you meet me. But I still hoped that in a way you would be glad to see me. And then I walked in from the street, and you sat there waiting, hard and afraid. Afraid of me. We talked about what the weather had been like here. And then you said you had to catch your train. What did I do, Mother, all those years ago, that was so horrible?

MRS. CALLIFER: You are imagining things.

JAMES: No, Mother, there's usually a moment when parents begin to speak the truth to their children. It's been a long time delayed in our case.

MRS. CALLIFER: There never is such a moment. First the children are too young, and then the parents are too old for truth. I'm too old, James. Please.

JAMES: Then there is a truth.

MRS. CALLIFER: You'll have to go somewhere else to find it.

JAMES: I've looked for it already in some strange places.

MRS. CALLIFER: Yes?

JAMES: Once a week I go to a doctor and he injects me with methedrine, and I talk and talk.

MRS. CALLIFER: What good does that do?

JAMES: None yet. I tell him how my marriage broke and about my childhood, all I can remember. How my parents avoided me. Don't we have to learn love from our parents, like we learn to walk? You taught me to walk, but I've no idea what love is.

MRS. CALLIFER: You are wrong, James. You had love, so much love, my dear, until— (*She stops.*)

JAMES: Until what?

47

MRS. CALLIFER: I'm very tired, James. Please don't ask me tonight.

JAMES: I'll be gone tomorrow.

MRS. CALLIFER: We shouldn't have buried it; but now it's been buried such a long time, I don't know what it would look like.

JAMES: Mother, please. Shut your eyes and think I'm your child. There's something I don't understand, and I fear it, and I've come running.

MRS. CALLIFER: I've got to protect Henry.

JAMES: He's dead.

MRS. CALLIFER (*with a moan of pain*): Can't I be loyal to him for a few hours?

JAMES: It won't affect him.

MRS. CALLIFER: How do we know?

JAMES: I don't. I thought you did. (*He scrambles to his feet; his appeal is over and the bitterness returns.*) Don't worry. I won't ask you again. I dreamed for a moment you were my mother and I was your child, and I went to my mother with my fear. For now, I thought, my father isn't here, to be protected. Doesn't a child deserve protection too? (*Mrs. Callifer's head is bowed, and she is crying.*) I pretended to myself you were a mother like other mothers, and I was a child like any other child. Somebody you can comfort so easily, saying, "They are only shadows," and lighting a lamp, or giving him a toy spade to dig with—

MRS. CALLIFER (*with an elderly whimper of pain*): **Oh, do** you remember that toy spade? You were only six.

JAMES (*in excitement*): What do you mean?

MRS. CALLIFER: We can be hurt by such silly things. **You** spoke as though you never liked that spade, but you **were so** happy . . .

JAMES (*almost with fear*): I've never remembered **anything** as far back as that before. (*It is as though at last a whole world of memory is at the door of the mind.*)

MRS. CALLIFER: Let me go now. (*He makes no move to stop her.*) We can talk again—one day. Good-bye. (*She kisses his cheek.*) I don't suppose I shall be up when you go. (*She goes out.*)

And James makes no reply—he is staring at a toy spade that has swum up from the unknown past.

The door opens, and Anne comes in, in her dressing-gown. He doesn't see her. A long pause.

ANNE: Hullo.

JAMES (*turning quickly*): What do you want?

ANNE: That's an awfully difficult question to answer.

JAMES: What have you been doing out there?

ANNE: Listening.

JAMES: That's very wrong.

ANNE: Don't you ever do anything that's wrong?

49

JAMES: Yes, and sometimes I can't even remember what.

ANNE: Are uncles prohibited?

JAMES: Huh?

ANNE: As husbands?

JAMES: Yes.

ANNE: It's a pity. We'd get on very well together. You see, I don't know what love is either.

JAMES: You certainly have been listening.

ANNE: I'm curious by nature. I'd make a good detective. I mean—when the vow is finished. You can't expect a detective to tell the truth.

JAMES: Why were you listening?

ANNE: I was on the prowl and I heard voices. There's an awful lot to be found out everywhere.

JAMES: Everywhere?

ANNE: I'm frightened of the laurel walk, too. After dark. That's why I wouldn't take the water to Spot. I kept on thinking, "Out, out, damned spot." Because if there were ghosts, the potting shed might be haunted—(*James's attention is caught*) and you can't be quite certain of anything, can you?

JAMES: Why—the potting shed?

ANNE: Something awful happened there once.

JAMES: How do you know?

ANNE: I heard the gardener talking one day to a man who'd come for seedlings. He was talking about Potter, the gardener they used to have here years ago. He said, "I always thought Mr. Callifer was pleased when old Potter passed on." He meant died, you know. The other man said why, and Willis—he's the gardener now—said, "I reckon it was because he was here when that thing happened. He saw it all. Right here. Something shocking it was." I don't like the smell of mould, do you?

JAMES (*letting it sink in*): Something shocking . . .

ANNE: I expect they hushed it up, but that's why I thought, "Out, damned spot."

JAMES: I don't believe you.

ANNE: You must. Because of my vow.

JAMES: But it needn't have anything to do with me. I couldn't have done anything very terrible. Not at that age.

ANNE: He said, "Poor Master James."

JAMES: I remember nothing. Nothing. I don't look like someone who'd do anything as shocking as that, do I?

ANNE (*remembering her vow, looks at him carefully before replying*): No. You don't look like that, but I don't suppose people usually do. Everything is possible, isn't it?

CURTAIN

Act Two

Act Two
SCENE ONE

A month has passed. This is the living room of James Calli-
fer's lodgings at Nottingham. The furniture is his landlady's,
and could belong to nobody but a landlady: the bobbed
fringes of the sage green tablecloth, the sideboard with a mir-
ror, the glass biscuit box with a silver top, the Marcus Stone
engravings.

The door of the living room is open and voices can be
heard outside. Dr. Kreuzer enters, followed by Corner. Kreu-
zer is an elderly man with a tough, kindly face, obviously in a
state of anxiety. Corner is in the early thirties—thin and
nervous, a heavy smoker. Kreuzer wears an overcoat. Corner
is obviously at home. He clears newspapers from a chair for
Kreuzer.

CORNER: Come in, Dr. Kreuzer. Callifer's spoken of you
many a time.

KREUZER: You're Mr. Corner, aren't you? He's spoken of you,
too. The only real reporter the *Globe* has, he says.

CORNER: He doesn't say it to me. Sit down and wait, Dr.
Kreuzer. He must be back soon.

55

KREUZER: Haven't you seen him this morning?

CORNER: Not since breakfast. He said he had an appointment with you and methedrine. Sounds like a girl.

KREUZER: Not unlike, Mr. Corner. It makes a shy man talk. Callifer left me two hours ago. I must get hold of him. Have you a phone here?

CORNER: I wouldn't use it if I were you. It's a party line. Unless it's an emergency. Is it?

KREUZER: I don't know. I wish I did.

CORNER: What's happened?

KREUZER: He took something from my desk which I need back.

CORNER: Stole it?

KREUZER: No, no. A patient doesn't steal. It was my fault. (*He can't keep still. He gets up and walks around.*)

CORNER: What's wrong with him, Doctor?

KREUZER: I don't know.

CORNER: We all have moods.

KREUZER: Some moods are blacker than others.

CORNER: But he's good at his job. Or he wouldn't have stayed five years on the *Globe*.

KREUZER (*hardly listening*): When he takes a walk, where does he go?

CORNER: He used to go along the Trent when he had the dog. Or down to the goose market.

KREUZER: Hasn't he got the dog still?

CORNER: It ran away.

KREUZER: I'm sorry.

CORNER: He didn't seem to mind.

KREUZER: I wonder why he didn't tell me about it?

CORNER: Perhaps it wasn't important enough.

KREUZER: You live with him, Mr. Corner. What is important to him?

CORNER: I wouldn't know.

The door opens and James enters. He is still in an exalted state from the methedrine.

JAMES: Well, well—so you've hunted me down to my digs, Dr. Kreuzer. Digs—the word sounds like an animal's hole, doesn't it?

KREUZER: I wanted to see the kind of place you live in. It's a bit anonymous.

JAMES: A lodging for the night. The slow, dark hours. For me and my colleague, Corner. I'm glad you've met Corner. You read him every day. (*He picks up one of the newspapers.*) Listen to this—"Counselor Worm's Tour in Europe. Counselor Worm, who has just returned from a visit to Paris and Le Touquet, reports that the French feel deeply." The text is Corner's. The headlines are mine. I wanted to call it "A

57

Worm's-Eye View," but the chief sub-editor is against gaiety on the *Globe*.

CORNER: There's a telegram for you on the mantelpiece. He's always like this, Doctor, after he's seen you. She seems to be a nice girl, methedrine.

KREUZER: She can let a man down, too.

JAMES (*reading telegram*): It's from my mother. I suppose she's fetching Anne from school. It's just as I told you. This is the way they always visit me. Between trains. Lucky Nottingham is a junction. In the summer term I never see them; I suppose there's a better connection.

KREUZER: You're still excited, Callifer.

JAMES: Well, I've remembered something, haven't I? Did you ever have a toy spade, Corner? Doctor, are all your patients as anxious as I am to be cured?

KREUZER: They don't come until they want it enough.

JAMES: You should try him, Corner. You might stop throwing away half-smoked cigarettes at three and tenpence a packet. It might lend color to your reports of council meetings. A jab in the arms, a little nausea for a few seconds, and then—a desire to talk till the cows come home. What time do cows come home, Corner?

CORNER: It depends what you mean by cows. Callifer, if your mum's coming I'm going to my room. She always makes me feel like a cub reporter. Good-bye, Dr. Kreuzer.

KREUZER: Good-bye, Mr. Corner.

CORNER: I'll come for a shot in the arm myself one day.

Corner leaves. There is a short silence.

KREUZER: It's not only the methedrine which is exciting you.

JAMES: Why are you really here, Doctor?

KREUZER: I have a sense that I failed you today.

JAMES: You? Why?

KREUZER: You came to me with a kind of hope.

JAMES: I went away with a kind of hope, too.

KREUZER: We are not in my consulting room now. Perhaps you can talk to me more easily here.

JAMES: I've talked myself dry. Six months of talking. It hasn't got us far. Perhaps what I really need is action.

KREUZER: What action? What's that you're playing with?

JAMES: A toy. Something I picked up. We've been talking about childhood so long, you mustn't mind if I start playing with toys again. Not a spade this time. We've exhausted the spade.

KREUZER: Oh, no we haven't. You brought it up—and there we stopped. You had an important engagement. Don't you remember?

59

The Potting Shed

JAMES: There's no point in the spade. Every child has one. Or so I've read. I've read a lot about childhood. It helped to fill the gap.

KREUZER: How?

JAMES: I built up an imaginary childhood. That plot of garden. Seed evelopes with coloured pictures that one bought in shops. But there were more important seeds, Doctor, not in packets. Like the best wine of a region that comes from unlabelled bottles. Seeds in old cardboard boxes. One stole them from the gardener and planted them in the ground and one never knew what flower or vegetable would grow. The boxes lay on the earth in the potting shed. (*He stops abruptly.*)

KREUZER: Go on.

JAMES: I can't. (*He gets up.*) It's too hot in here.

KREUZER: Sit down. I'll open the window. (*He opens the window behind James's head, and shivers slightly in the cold air. James remains standing.*) In what book did you read about the potting shed?

JAMES (*agitated*): I don't know. I can't remember.

KREUZER: Perhaps it was a real potting shed.

JAMES: Yes. A real potting shed. And a month ago I began to walk down the laurel path towards it. It was dark. I was carrying water for my dog. And I didn't have the courage even to come within sight of the door. Father, can't you tell me—

KREUZER: You called me Father.

James: So I did. But he's dead, and he'll never tell me now.

Kreuzer: Relax. Try not to worry. Talk about something else. Forget the potting shed.

James: I had. All those years. (*He sits.*) But you can't forget forever what exists. Sooner or later, a smell, a touch—our footsteps make such a pattern over the world in forty years, they'd have to tread the same path again sooner or later. Wouldn't they, Doctor?

Kreuzer: I believe there's nothing human which can't somehow with patience be recalled.

James: And do you believe in anything that isn't human?

Kreuzer: No, I don't believe. Sometimes I doubt my disbelief.

James: What could have happened that was so terrible it wiped out all memory? I was a boy, Doctor. What a boy can do is very limited.

Kreuzer: Perhaps it was something done to you.

James: Then why the disgrace? Oh, I know some parents make a fuss about the little sexual games children play. Not my parents, though. It can't have been anything like that. They were never worried by anything human.

Kreuzer: That word "human" again.

James: Well, God was taboo. My father had killed that superstition for his generation. Poor Father! I'm glad he didn't realize how it was beginning to return. Like memory. We

61

were not allowed ghost stories, either. Do you believe in ghosts, Doctor?

KREUZER: No.

JAMES: Or the soul?

KREUZER: I've never understood what the word means.

JAMES: If I had a child, I wouldn't forbid it fairy stories. They might develop the sense of hope. If a pumpkin can turn into a coach, even this dreary room, that tablecloth, those awful ornaments, could be a palace, with limitless corridors.

KREUZER: Did you ever want a child?

JAMES: No. I didn't want to create new convicts for a prison. To have a child you need hope.

KREUZER: There seems to be plenty of hope, then, around us. Judging by the birth rate.

JAMES: There should be another word for that simple sort of hope.

KREUZER: It's enough for most of us.

JAMES: Doctor, I'm not sneering. I want it to be enough for me too. Why isn't it? What happened to me—in that shed?

KREUZER: For six months now I've been trying to find out, and you haven't given me a clue.

JAMES (*pleading for hope*): I was beginning to remember.

KREUZER: Yes. Outside that door. But what happened when

the door shut behind you? Was there a lock? A bolt? A catch? Answer me quickly.

JAMES (*in a low voice*): I can't remember.

KREUZER: Were you alone?

JAMES: I don't know.

KREUZER: Think aloud. Invent. Tell a story—any story—a fairy story. Whatever comes into your head.

JAMES: Our Father methedrine, hallowed be Thy name. (*He puts his head in his hands.*)

KREUZER: You've seen many other sheds like that, haven't you, besides the one you fear so? Describe them to me. Anything. The spades leaning against the wall. The smell of mould.

A pause, while James tries to remember, to invent.

JAMES: It's as if there were only one place like that in the world. The walk was called the dark walk. The door was never painted.

KREUZER: Are you inventing?

JAMES: I think so. I don't know. I kept my spade in there, with the real spades. In that way it seemed to be no longer a toy. But that was years before. Something made a pattern on the path as I walked, like a snake crawling beside me.

KREUZER: A snake?

JAMES: No, not a snake. I don't know. When I came in sight

63

of the door my heart was beating. I stopped to get my breath. My head was aching too, but I wasn't unhappy any more. Just frightened.

KREUZER: You'd been unhappy? (*James pays no attention to the question.*) Was somebody waiting for you?

JAMES: Yes, or something. I don't know. I can't remember. That damned door shuts it all out. (*Despairingly*): Doctor, we can go on for a lifetime like this, I'll never get through that door.

KREUZER: And when you came out again?

JAMES: I don't believe I ever came out. Sometimes I think I'm still lying there.

KREUZER: Lying?

JAMES: Oh, it was only the first word that came. I'm tired, Doctor, and my mother will be here any moment now.

KREUZER: You are frightened of making an effort to remember. I can't cure you. Perhaps there's nothing to cure.

JAMES: What do you mean?

KREUZER: I can only cure the irrational, the exaggerated, the abnormal. If a man is melancholy because he's lost his leg, I'm not called in. He has good reason.

JAMES: You think I may have reason?

KREUZER: Yes. But what happened behind that door to give you the reason—the mind boggles at that.

JAMES: So we give up? Right. It was my last fling, too.

KREUZER (*apprehensively and sharply*): Don't be a bigger coward than you need be.

JAMES: Trying to make me angry, Doctor? You can't. My plan needs courage.

KREUZER: I was just talking, Callifer, to make *you* talk. I never give a patient up.

JAMES: Has no one given you up?

KREUZER (*after a pause, unwillingly*): Yes, one.

JAMES: He got tired of it?

KREUZER: Yes.

JAMES: Did he find another cure?

KREUZER: Not what I can admit is a cure. Perhaps this may interest you. He killed himself.

JAMES: Oh. (*The words have struck home.*)

KREUZER: He was my son.

JAMES: I'm sorry.

KREUZER: He wouldn't be treated by anyone else. I tried to make him, but he was afraid. He was never afraid of me. I had to go and tell his mother. We hadn't met for years. She took it badly.

JAMES: How long ago?

KREUZER: Ten years. I swore then I'd never leave a case unfinished. Even if a patient tried to give me up. They often do.

65

The Potting Shed

Somewhere below, the front doorbell rings.

JAMES: My mother, Doctor Kreuzer.

KREUZER: Before I go— (*He holds out his hand.*)

JAMES: I don't understand.

KREUZER: You acted very quickly. I suppose it was when I turned to telephone. I forgot to examine my desk before you left. My tablets, please.

JAMES: Suppose I won't give them to you?

KREUZER: It's not very important. I'm trying to save you from a stomach ache, that's all. They're not poisonous.

JAMES: Then why did you follow me here?

KREUZER: I couldn't allow a patient to leave me ever again in that state of mind.

The door opens and Corner lets in Mrs. Callifer.

CORNER: Here's your mother, Callifer. (*He goes.*)

JAMES (*handing over the bottle*): Here they are.

MRS. CALLIFER: James—

JAMES: Welcome, Mother.

MRS. CALLIFER: Is Anne here?

JAMES: No.

MRS. CALLIFER: I lost her at the barrier. I'm sorry, James, interrupting—

66

JAMES: No, we've finished. Quite finished. This is Dr. Kreuzer, Mother.

They shake hands.

MRS. CALLIFER: He's not ill, is he, Dr. Kreuzer?

JAMES: He's not that kind of doctor. He makes me talk, that's all.

MRS. CALLIFER: Is that supposed to be a good thing nowadays?

KREUZER (*picking up his case*): Your generation believed in letting sleeping dogs lie, Mrs. Callifer.

MRS. CALLIFER: Was that so wrong?

KREUZER: You were clever at keeping them asleep, but sometimes they wake up your children.

MRS. CALLIFER (*to James*): Do you think I ought to go back to the station?

JAMES: Anne's old enough. She knows her way.

MRS. CALLIFER: I can't think how I lost her. She went ahead while I collected the luggage. She said she'd wait at the barrier.

KREUZER: Well, good-bye, Callifer. Same time next week?

JAMES: It's no use, Doctor. We've failed.

KREUZER: I told you. I never give up.

JAMES (*seeking an excuse*): I'm sorry, but I can't afford to play at this any longer.

67

KREUZER: There'll be no charge.

Mrs. Callifer can feel the conflict between the two men, *though she cannot understand it.*

MRS. CALLIFER: If it's a question of money—

KREUZER: It isn't. It's a question of courage.

JAMES: No. Only a question of hope.

KREUZER: Callifer, I've had this conversation before with someone else. I beg you . . .

JAMES: I shall do nothing foolishly. I'm quite calm. You can feel my pulse. (*He holds out his hand.*)

KREUZER (*turning hopelessly away and picking up his bag*): It would be useless. I should feel only the methedrine. Mrs. Callifer, if only you would help him.

JAMES: Look, I don't want my mother troubled.

KREUZER: I thought you didn't know what love was? Very well, then, but I'll phone you in the morning. Good-bye, Mrs. Callifer. (*He goes out.*)

JAMES: He's a good man.

MRS. CALLIFER: What did he mean? How could I help? What were you talking about before I came?

JAMES: A potting shed where something happened. Mother, why did you leave my uncle out as well as me when my father was dying?

MRS. CALLIFER: There had been a quarrel years ago.

JAMES (*sitting down at his desk*): I can't remember his face.

MRS. CALLIFER: I wish you'd give up trying. He belongs to the past, James. Like your father and me. Old years are like old people. You should let them get weaker and weaker. Age is not pretty or graceful except in books. Leave old years alone, James.

JAMES: They won't leave me alone. (*A noise on the stairs.*) Oh, I think the truant has turned up. (*The door opens and Anne comes in. She is in her school uniform. She tries to slip in with a certain airy unobtrusiveness.*)

ANNE: Good afternoon, Uncle James.

JAMES: Hello, Anne.

ANNE: Where's Spot?

MRS. CALLIFER: Where have you been, Anne? You said you'd wait at the barrier.

ANNE: I did.

MRS. CALLIFER: You weren't there. I looked for you.

ANNE: Somebody told me you were waiting outside. So I went outside and I didn't find you, and then I took the wrong bus.

MRS. CALLIFER: Where have you been, Anne?

ANNE: I told you. Nowhere.

JAMES: Nothing and nowhere. It's the Callifer touch.

MRS. CALLIFER: I thought you were such a truthful girl.

ANNE: Oh, that was weeks ago.

MRS. CALLIFER: What do you mean?

ANNE: My vow is over. I can tell as many lies as I want to now.

MRS. CALLIFER: But you oughtn't to want to.

ANNE: You have to, if people ask too many questions, or if you want to lure somebody to a certain house at a certain hour—

MRS. CALLIFER: What on earth are you talking about now?

ANNE: I can tell Uncle James. I can't tell you.

MRS. CALLIFER: Why not?

ANNE: You have grandmother eyes.

JAMES: What are they?

ANNE: Old and upright.

JAMES: And mine?

ANNE: Oh, your eyes don't say anything. They just look away. Some peoples' eyes are always saying, "Cleanliness is next to godliness" or "*Virtus laudata crescit.*"

JAMES: *Virtus* . . . ?

ANNE: It's the school motto. "Virtue grows by praise," and whenever they say anything nice they expect the virtue to grow. Automatically. Like watering radishes. Where *is* Spot, Uncle?

MRS. CALLIFER: Anne, I asked you—

70

JAMES: He ran away.

ANNE: There ought to be paw prints as well as finger prints.

MRS. CALLIFER: She's talking a lot of nonsense to hide something.

ANNE: Where did you see Spot last, Uncle?

JAMES: I don't know. He was a very quiet dog. I hardly knew
when he was there.

ANNE: You could advertise.

JAMES: I expect he's happier where he is.

MRS. CALLIFER: Can't you see the child's play-acting? Anne,
what have you been up to?

ANNE: Didn't I tell you that I'd make a good detective? When
my vow was over. Any moment now you'll hear a ring and
that will be the answer to all the trouble.

JAMES: Who's going to ring, Anne?

ANNE: Mrs. Potter.

JAMES: Who's Mrs. Potter?

ANNE: Potter's wife. Yesterday I sent her a telegram.

JAMES: It's quite a habit of yours.

ANNE: Well, you came, didn't you, when I telegraphed? And
so, I expect, will Mrs. Potter.

MRS. CALLIFER: We are on our way to Wild Grove, Anne. We
have to catch a train. In three-quarters of an hour.

ANNE: Wild Grove can wait. I've just sent them a telegram too, that you'd been detained on urgent business. The real detective work came first, finding out that Mrs. Potter hadn't passed on. And where she lived. And when I found that out, everything was easy. Even the telegram. Of course she has quite a journey. We may have to wait for hours and hours, but it will be worth it, won't it, because she'll tell us what Potter saw.

JAMES: I'm just beginning to understand.

MRS. CALLIFER (*to James*): What's the child done?

JAMES: Perhaps what Dr. Kreuzer couldn't do.

A bell rings.

ANNE: There. I told you.

Pause while they listen.

MRS. CALLIFER: But Potter's dead.

ANNE: This is Mrs. Potter.

MRS. CALLIFER: What did you put in the telegram?

ANNE: "Dying. You can relieve a mind in torment. Come tea-time Thursday." I signed it "Callifer."

MRS. CALLIFER: Anne!

ANNE: Well, we are dying, aren't we, all of us?

JAMES: There were no lies in that telegram.

The bell rings again.

72

ANNE: Shall I go? (*She puts her hand on James's.*) Your hand, Uncle. It's shaking. You're afraid.

JAMES: No, no. It's the methedrine.

ANNE: I'll answer the door.

MRS. CALLIFER: No.

ANNE: I will.

JAMES: No. Stop where you are.

ANNE: You *are* afraid.

JAMES: That's what Dr. Kreuzer said. (*The bell rings a third time, impatiently. Turning round to the door*): Don't be so impatient. Can't you wait a few seconds longer on the door-step? You've been waiting for thirty years.

A long pause. No further ring.

ANNE: She's gone. We'll never know now.

The door opens and Corner enters.

CORNER: There's a woman at the door, Callifer. She says—

MRS. CALLIFER: Please tell her there's no one at home.

CORNER: She says she has an urgent telegram. From you, Callifer.

MRS. CALLIFER: Please tell her it was a mistake, Mr. Corner. A child's silly prank. Here, give her this for her fare.

JAMES: No. Let her come in.

73

MRS. CALLIFER: You'll only hear a lot of nonsense. Fairy stories, James. (*She is between him and the door.*) Mr. Corner, my son's excited by his treatment. Send her away. (*Corner hesitates.*) He's not in a fit state.

JAMES: She's come to see me, Corner. Not my mother. I'll fetch her if you won't. (*Corner looks at the two of them, shrugs and goes out.*) Mother, you stood in front of a door like this once before. But not again.

MRS. CALLIFER: What's the use, James? She wasn't there. She's only heard stories, exaggerated stories, Potter's stories. She knows nothing.

JAMES: Then tell me yourself. All you know. In your words. Before she comes.

MRS. CALLIFER: It was so long ago.

JAMES: I'll send her away if you'll tell.

MRS. CALLIFER: I promised your father.

JAMES: He's dead.

MRS. CALLIFER: Can't I keep a promise to the dead?

JAMES: Why should you if they're really dead? You won't be reproached by a bit of bone. Mother, it's you or Mrs. Potter.

A small, white-haired, scared woman enters. She is over seventy years old, and her face is wrinkled and country-like. She gives a frightened little nod and beck towards Mrs. Callifer.

MRS. POTTER: You won't remember me, ma'am.

MRS. CALLIFER: Oh yes, I remember you very well.

JAMES: I'm Mr. Callifer.

MRS. POTTER: I was expecting a sick gentleman from the telegram. Are you Master John?

JAMES: No, I'm James.

MRS. POTTER (*uneasily*): Oh.

JAMES: Come in, sit down, Mrs. Potter. (*She sits defensively on the very edge of the chair, looking nervously at Mrs. Callifer.*) I want to ask you some questions, Mrs. Potter. There's something I have to find out.

MRS. POTTER: What sort of questions, Master James?

JAMES: Do you remember the summer of 1925?

MRS. POTTER: All summers seem alike to me now, sir. Only warmer in those days.

JAMES: This was a different summer from all the others. Do you remember my uncle, Father Callifer?

MRS. POTTER: Oh, yes, sir, a fine young man. You and he were very close. That is, before—

JAMES: Before?

MRS. POTTER (*evasively*): There's always trouble in families, sir.

JAMES: Mrs. Potter, one day that summer your husband went to the potting shed and found somebody, something, there. (*A pause. Mrs. Potter stares at her hands.*) It was something that shocked him very much. He wouldn't have kept it dark from you, would he?

75

MRS. POTTER: Potter and me never had secrets.

JAMES: What did he tell you?

MRS. POTTER: It's a long, long time ago, sir.

JAMES: But you remember it.

MRS. POTTER: Potter said don't tell a soul, and I never have. For your poor dad's sake.

JAMES: My father's dead. You can tell me now.

MRS. POTTER (*pleading*): But you know, sir, already. What's the good of raking around?

JAMES: I've forgotten everything that happened that day.

MRS. POTTER: You couldn't, sir, not— (*She stops again.*)

JAMES: Mrs. Potter, I didn't send you that telegram, but my mind *is* in torment. I've *got* to know.

MRS. POTTER: Ask your mother. Me, I'm only Potter's wife. Potter's widow. What'd *I* know about it?

JAMES: Well, Mother? (*His mother turns away.*) You see, my mother won't tell me. You are the last chance I have, Mrs. Potter. If you owe anything to us . . .

MRS. POTTER: I owe everything to the Callifers. But if your mother doesn't want you to know . . .

JAMES: Weren't we friends in those days, Mrs. Potter?

MRS. POTTER: You was always my favourite, Master James. It wasn't any fault of yours what happened. You were a dear boy to me. If your father had let you alone—

76

JAMES: I haven't asked you for anything in thirty years, but I'm begging you now—

Mrs. Potter looks at Mrs. Callifer.

MRS. POTTER: But your mother—

MRS. CALLIFER: All right. I'll tell you. You had an accident in the potting shed.

JAMES: An accident?

MRS. CALLIFER: You slipped and fell. You were unconscious when Potter found you. And afterwards—it made you strange.

JAMES: Mad?

MRS. CALLIFER: Not exactly mad. You didn't get on with your father. Family life wasn't good for you.

JAMES: Is that all?

MRS. CALLIFER: All except Potter's fairy stories.

JAMES: Then I want the fairy stories.

MRS. POTTER: They weren't fairy stories, Mrs. Callifer. Potter was no liar. Your husband knew that. That's why he sent him away.

MRS. CALLIFER: He was too old for the work. My husband gave him a good pension.

MRS. POTTER: Oh, it was a good pension, but his heart was in his garden, and it killed him.

MRS. CALLIFER: He spread stories.

77

MRS. POTTER: It was the truth.

MRS. CALLIFER: How could it be?

MRS. POTTER: It's not the first time. There was Lazarus. They buried *him*.

ANNE: Who was Lazarus?

MRS. CALLIFER: Someone in a book.

MRS. POTTER (*angrily*): A book you Callifers aren't allowed to read. All right. I'll tell you how it was, Master James. It was dinnertime. Potter was late. Near two o'clock. I knew something was wrong as soon as he came in. He had a coffin face. It was bad for Potter because he found you first.

JAMES: He found me?

MRS. POTTER: He lifted you down, poor boy.

JAMES: Lifted me— (*He sits down at the desk.*)

MRS. POTTER: You were hanging there, sir. You'd used a cord from the playroom. He cut you down.

JAMES: Was I—

MRS. POTTER: There wasn't any life in you, sir.

MRS. CALLIFER: No! (*She makes a motion of protest.*)

MRS. POTTER: Forgive me, ma'am, but it's what Potter said.

JAMES: (*as though it were a real question, and he half expects the answer to be no*): But I am here? This is my room.

78

MRS. POTTER: Potter did all he could. He was a great swimmer once, sir, and he knew all about artificial respirationing. It wasn't any use, he said. Your heart was stopped. He was always a truthful man.

JAMES: Last week I cut my hand. It bled.

MRS. POTTER: Potter left the door open, and he looked up and saw your uncle was there. "Master James has killed himself," Potter said. You were stretched out there on the ground and you had no more breath, Potter said, than a dead fish.

MRS. CALLIFER: James, it was all a mistake. You don't take this seriously, James?

JAMES: What's your story, Mother? You've kept it dark a long while.

MRS. CALLIFER: There was no story to tell. We didn't want you to remember how foolish you'd been. You were in a coma from shock. When the doctor came he revived you.

MRS. POTTER: Not the doctor. Potter left you with your uncle, Master James.

MRS. CALLIFER: Potter did better than he knew. Perhaps he did save your life.

MRS. POTTER: Potter never thought that. He was beyond human aid, Potter said.

JAMES: Mother, where's my uncle now? (*Pause.*) You may as well tell me.

MRS. CALLIFER: Even if I knew where he was I wouldn't tell

79

you. What use could he be to you in the state you'd find him in?

JAMES: Mother, you can't hush *him* up. There are directories where one can find a priest's address.

ANNE (*coming forward*): I'll find it for you. (*They all turn and look at her.*) It will be a lot easier than finding Mrs. Potter.

JAMES: No! Leave this to me.

CURTAIN

Act Two
SCENE TWO

Act Two
SCENE TWO

Evening. The sitting room in Father Callifer's presbytery in an East Anglian town. There is something in its homelessness that reminds us of James Callifer's lodgings in Nottingham. Only instead of pictures by Marcus Stone there are a hideous Sacred Heart, a dreary print of a Mother and Child belonging to Raphael's most sugary period. There is a crucifix on the dresser, instead of a biscuit-box. One feels that all has been inherited from another priest. They are part of a second-hand uniform. There are two doors, one opening on another part of the house, the other into a little drab hall.

There are the remains of an evening meal on a tray on the table in the sitting room. A bottle of cheap altar wine is all but finished.

Miss Connolly, Father Callifer's housekeeper, has just let a man into the hall. He wears a raincoat over his shoulders. In the half-dark, for the only light comes from the street outside, we do not at first recognize James Callifer. Miss Connolly is a hard-faced woman of over fifty. She has known

*many other priests in her time and has learned only too well
to distinguish between the office and the man.*

Miss Connolly: For what would you be wanting the father
at this hour? There's proper times for confession. They are
on the church board. Is it confession?

James: No.

Miss Connolly: Instruction? I doubt if he's in a fit state
after his supper. He's easily tired.

James: So I've heard.

Miss Connolly: You shouldn't believe all you hear. Where
do you come from?

James: A long way. Just tell him—

Miss Connolly: I can't let you have a light. The bulb's
burned out, and I haven't a spare one in the house.

James: I don't mind the darkness.

Miss Connolly: I promise nothing, mind. You should have
come in the morning. He's best after breakfast.

James: I won't be here. I'm only passing through.

Miss Connolly: Then what kind of instruction are you expecting?

James: Instruction was *your* word.

*She goes out impatiently, shutting the door behind her,
crosses the sitting room and goes out by the other door. Now
we can hardly make out James at all. He sits quietly until*

the others return. When he hears them speaking, he approaches the door and listens. We hear their voices first on the stairs outside the sitting room, or rather Miss Connolly's voice.

MISS CONNOLLY (*voice*): And when can I find you capable? Answer me that. (*Father Callifer enters, followed by Miss Connolly. He has a stubbly, worn face with bloodshot eyes: a dirty wisp of a Roman collar has been made by twisting and folding a handkerchief round the top of his shirt.*) I'm waiting for an answer. (*The priest goes to the mantelpiece and places his hands on it as though for support. He has his back to Miss Connolly and the audience.*) They'd have written to the Bishop long before this if I'd let them. (*A pause.*) Don't think they haven't learnt what happened in your last parish and the one before that. If I hadn't begged them time and again to give you a chance, if only for my sake—

CALLIFER (*not turning*): Your sake?

MISS CONNOLLY: I've been the priest's housekeeper here for twenty years and never had a breath of scandal before. But unless you give me your solemn honest-to-God promise you'll keep off the liquor I'll not be preventing them any longer writing to the Bishop.

CALLIFER: Let them write.

MISS CONNOLLY: If they do it will be the end of you. You won't find another bishop to take you.

CALLIFER (*swinging suddenly round*): Do you think I'd mind that? Let them take away my faculties. Don't threaten a convict with the loss of his chains.

MISS CONNOLLY: Speak lower if you don't want to advertise your shame to a stranger.

CALLIFER: Go and fetch the man, whoever he is.

MISS CONNOLLY: I'm going to have my say first. Here they want a priest with the faith in him. Don't turn away and pretend you don't understand.

CALLIFER: Fetch him in, I say.

MISS CONNOLLY: You and I have got to have this out once and for all. (*With a slight softening*): It's for your sake I'm speaking.

CALLIFER: I say the Mass every Sunday at eight-thirty and on week-days at seven for those who care to come. There aren't many of them. What else do you want of me?

MISS CONNOLLY: Oh, you stand at the altar all right, gabbling your way through as quickly as possible to get at your breakfast. But you don't believe a word you are saying.

CALLIFER: How do you know?

MISS CONNOLLY: In a life like mine you get an ear for such things.

CALLIFER: Yes, I suppose so.

MISS CONNOLLY: You should have heard poor Father Murphy and the beautiful voice he had. He wouldn't have read other men's sermons because he had no thoughts of his own.

CALLIFER: I can tell he never preached to you on charity.

MISS CONNOLLY: I found your new hiding place this morning. (*Callifer turns his back on her and moves away. More gently*): Father, what kind of a priest are you?

CALLIFER: A priest who does his job. I say the Mass, I hear confessions, if anyone has a stomach ache in the night, don't I go to him? Who has ever asked for me and I haven't come?

MISS CONNOLLY: Miss Alexander.

CALLIFER (*slowly, with shame*): Yes, you would remind me of that.

MISS CONNOLLY: I couldn't wake you. I had to say next day you were sick. Sick!

CALLIFER: Miss Connolly, you've looked after a lot of priests. You take it as your right to speak your mind to them. And me—you expect me to serve you, all of you, every day for twenty-four hours. I mustn't be a man. I must be a priest. And in return, after Mass you give me coffee and eggs (in all these years you've never learnt how to make coffee) and you make my bed. You keep my two rooms clean—or nearly. (*He runs his finger along the mantelpiece.*) I don't ask you for any more than you are paid to do.

MISS CONNOLLY: The people here have a right to a priest with the faith.

CALLIFER: Faith. They want a play-actor. They want snow-white hair, high collars, clean vestments (who pays the cleaner?—not their sixpence), and they want a voice that's never husky with the boredom of saying the same words day after day. All right. Let them write to the Bishop. Do you think I want to get up every morning at six in time to make my meditation before Mass? Meditation on what? The reason why I'm going on with this slave-labour? They give prisoners useless tasks, don't they, digging pits and filling them up again? Like mine.

MISS CONNOLLY: Speak low. You don't understand what you are saying, Father.

CALLIFER: Father! I hate the word. I had a brother who believed in nothing, and for thirty years now I have believed in nothing too. I used to pray, I used to love what you call God, and then my eyes were opened—to nothing. A father belongs to his children until they grow up and he's free of them. But these people will never grow up. They die children and leave children behind them. I'm condemned to being a father for life.

MISS CONNOLLY: I've never heard such words before out of a priest's mouth.

A pause.

CALLIFER: You wouldn't have heard them now if the bottle you found hadn't been empty.

MISS CONNOLLY: They say your breath smells in the confessional.

CALLIFER: And so do theirs. Of worse things. I'd rather smell of whisky than bad teeth.

MISS CONNOLLY: You're full of it now.

CALLIFER: Oh no, I'm empty. Quite empty. (*The door from*

86

the hall opens and James Callifer enters.) Who are you?

JAMES: Your nephew. If you are Father Callifer.

CALLIFER: My nephew? (*Pulling himself together*): Well, well, it's long since I've seen any of the family. I wouldn't have kept you waiting if I'd known. I thought you were just —well— You should have warned me you were coming. Miss Connolly—

MISS CONNOLLY: I can get the guest room ready right away.

JAMES: I'm not staying. I was only passing and I thought—

CALLIFER: The nearest town where you'll be comfortable is Wisbech. That's twenty miles away. You'd do much better to stay the night here.

MISS CONNOLLY: The sheets are ready aired.

CALLIFER (*he is unused to being a host; nobody has stayed in this house for years*): Have you dined? It would be no trouble, would it, Miss Connolly, you could—

MISS CONNOLLY: There's a couple of chops for tomorrow's lunch. It won't take a minute.

CALLIFER: Where are my manners? I forgot to introduce the two of you. This is my housekeeper, Miss Connolly. My nephew, John.

JAMES (*who does not correct him*): How do you do, Miss Connolly? I had food on the way. I just wanted to see you, have a word with you after all these years. Perhaps a drink.

87

The Potting Shed

CALLIFER (*watching Miss Connolly*): Of course you must have a drink. While Miss Connolly is getting your room ready. Sit down, my dear fellow, sit down. *That's* the only comfortable chair. Now, Miss Connolly, what have we in the house?

MISS CONNOLLY (*grudgingly*): There's a bit of sherry.

CALLIFER: Not at this hour.

MISS CONNOLLY: Maybe I can find some altar wine.

CALLIFER: Do. And bring a jug of water.

MISS CONNOLLY (*suspiciously*): What would you be wanting the water for?

CALLIFER: To temper the wine, Miss Connolly. (*Miss Connolly goes out with the supper tray.*) A good woman—in her way. And how's the bank?

JAMES: I work on a newspaper.

CALLIFER: Oh, I was thinking— But I haven't kept up. Were you at your poor father's funeral?

JAMES: Yes, but I wasn't invited.

CALLIFER: Nor was I, but you— (*He looks at him sharply.*)

JAMES: For the same reason. I'm James, Uncle, not John. A strange meeting, isn't it?—the first since that potting shed.

At this moment Miss Connolly enters with a tray. She puts it on the table.

MISS CONNOLLY: Is there anything else you'll be wanting?

CALLIFER: No. You can go to bed. I'll show my nephew up. (*She leaves.*) So you are James.

JAMES: Yes.

CALLIFER: I wish you hadn't come.

JAMES: Why?

CALLIFER: We were very close once. Do you remember?

JAMES: No.

CALLIFER: I'm glad. You won't find me so changed then.

JAMES: I couldn't help listening just now—you didn't lower your voice.

CALLIFER: That's honest, anyway. So we needn't pretend. You'll have some whisky? A reunion like this demands— (*He doesn't wait for an answer, but goes to his bookcase and draws out the first volume of the Catholic Encyclopedia and then the second. Behind it is a full bottle.*) Volume 2, C. to F. I can't offer you soda. She'd notice if I kept soda in the house. (*He pours out two very large glasses and drinks deeply of his own.*) Welcome to my home. Rather different from Wild Grove, isn't it? But then your father and I followed different ways. They say you can tell a man's character from his furnishings. (*James looks around.*) Yes, you can see mine standing all round you for yourself. What sort of rooms have you got, I wonder? They'll have told you at Wild Grove that I'm over fond of this. (*He raises his glass.*) But I do my job. Nobody can deny I do my job. Look at the pictures, the books. I keep up appearances, don't I? We are intelligent men, you and I. Look at that picture of the Sacred Heart. A Christmas

89

card made out of a medical textbook. (*He takes another long drink of whisky.*) Does John drink?

JAMES: A glass of wine with his meals.

CALLIFER: A lucky man. How does it go? "They scoff at scars who never felt a wound"?

JAMES: What's your wound, Uncle?

CALLIFER: My wound? Nothing serious. It's a difficult thing, though, practising a faith, day in, day out, when you don't believe one jot of it. Do you know that at night I still pray— to nothing, to that. (*He indicates the crucifix with his glass.*) I was teaching you to believe in that when your father interfered. How right he was.

JAMES: Right?

CALLIFER: He was a very clever man. Older and cleverer than I was. He took everything I told you and made fun of it. He made me a laughing stock before you. I had taught you about the Virgin birth and he cured you with physiology.

JAMES: Was that why I tried to kill myself?

CALLIFER: So you know about that, do you? He was a bit too rough. (*A pause.*) Fill your glass. We have to get through this bottle by twelve.

JAMES: Why by twelve?

CALLIFER: I have to say Mass in the morning. I abide by the rules. It's the least I can do.

JAMES: For who?

CALLIFER: For myself. (*He gives an unhappy laugh.*) I caught you there. You thought you had squeezed out a small drop of faith. But there isn't one drop.

As James is helping himself Miss Connolly enters. She has an old-fashioned kitchen alarm clock in her hand.

MISS CONNOLLY (*harshly*): I've set the alarm for six. (*She sees what they are drinking.*) So that's why you asked for the water. Where had you got that hidden?

JAMES: I brought it.

MISS CONNOLLY: I try so hard to keep him off the drink, and now you are sending him drunk to bed.

JAMES: I'm sorry. I needed the drink more than he did.

MISS CONNOLLY (*her harshness gone as she looks at the old man drooping in his chair*): You'll see he goes up to bed soon, won't you; he has to wake early. He works hard in his way. (*She pauses at the door.*) Do you know what he called himself just now? A convict. He said he was in prison. I'm the warder, I suppose. He hasn't any love or gratitude in him for the years he has been looked after.

JAMES: It's a terrible thing to have nothing in you.

MISS CONNOLLY: And I'd give my life for him. (*She goes out.*)

CALLIFER (*rousing himself*): I've made her angry again. Where's the point? I think I'll go to bed if you'll help me. What were we talking about when she came in?

91

JAMES: Have you really forgotten what happened?

CALLIFER: I've forgotten nothing. I don't like to remember, that's all. It was a terrible day for everybody. I was very angry with your father for the way he treated you. Of course he had reason, but it was a shocking thing for a boy to be brought to hang himself.

JAMES: What happened when you found me? I wasn't—dead, was I?

CALLIFER: How could you have been dead? Oh, Potter thought so. And so did I, perhaps. I put a dead leaf on your lips and it didn't move. But they have a word for that. It was a coma. Just a coma. The doctor said so.

JAMES: Tell me what you did.

CALLIFER: I prayed. You see, in those days I believed. I wish you hadn't come back. I'd forgotten what you looked like. I don't care to remember faces. When I shave, I shave without a mirror.

JAMES: Did the doctor bring me to?

CALLIFER: Oh, no. You were awake before he came.

JAMES: It isn't possible, is it, I mean—what Potter thought?

CALLIFER: If you were dead it would have been a miracle, and if it were a miracle God would exist. That hideous picture there would have a meaning. But if God existed, why should He take away His faith from me? I've served Him well. I go on serving Him. The saints have dark nights, but not for thirty years. They have moments when they remember what it felt like to believe.

JAMES: Do you remember nothing?

CALLIFER: I don't want to remember. You shouldn't have come.

JAMES: Tell me what you remember.

CALLIFER (*drinking*): The shed and you lying there and Potter struggling with your arms.

JAMES: And then?

CALLIFER: I prayed. I was a model priest, you see, with all the beliefs and conventions. Besides, I loved you. Yes, I remember now, how I loved you. I couldn't have a child, and I suppose you took his place. Let me have one more drink. (*He pours out a drink but does not drink.*) When I had you on my knees I remember a terrible pain—here. So terrible I don't think I could go through it again. It was just as though I was the one who was strangled—I could feel the cord round my neck. I couldn't breathe, I couldn't speak, I had to pray in my mind, and then your breath came back, and it was just as though I had died instead. So I went away to bury myself in rooms like this.

JAMES: What did you pray?

CALLIFER: It's so long ago.

JAMES: Try to remember.

CALLIFER: What difference would it make to you?

JAMES: I've been close to despair too.

CALLIFER (*changing the subject*): What made you remember me?

JAMES: Potter's widow.

CALLIFER: Is he dead? Poor fellow. And so you came to me? Do I look as though I could be of any use to anyone at all? (*Pause.*) It was an awful moment, finding you dead in that way.

JAMES: Dead?

CALLIFER: I mean you seemed to me dead.

JAMES: What did you do?

CALLIFER: I'd have given my life for you—but what could I do? I could only pray. I suppose I offered something in return. Something I valued—not spirits. I really thought I loved God in those days. I said—I said, "Let him live, God. I love him. Let him live. I will give you anything if you will let him live." But what had I got to give Him? I was a poor man. I said, "Take away what I love most. Take—take—" (*He can't remember.*)

JAMES: "Take away my faith but let him live"?

CALLIFER: Did you hear me?

JAMES: Yes. You were speaking a long way off, and I came towards you through a cave of darkness. I didn't want to come. I struggled not to come. But something pushed me to you.

CALLIFER: Something?

94

JAMES: Or somebody. (*Callifer begins to weep.*) Uncle, can I help?

CALLIFER: I even forgot what I said to Him, until you came. He answered my prayer, didn't He? He took my offer.

JAMES: Do you really believe . . .

CALLIFER: Look around you. Look at this room. It makes sense, doesn't it, now? (*He sweeps a glass onto the floor.*) You must forgive me. I'm tired and a little drunk. I haven't thought about that day for thirty years. Will you see me to my room? It's dark on the landing. (*He gets up, and then pauses and looks up at the hideous picture.*) I thought I had lost Him forever.

CURTAIN

Act Three

Act Three

The drawing room at Wild Grove. Evening. Mrs. Callifer has a book on her lap but she is not reading. Sara is facing an untidy pile of holly.

SARA (*picking up the holly*): It's a bad year for berries. (*She looks up at the cornice.*) I'll have to get the stepladder.

MRS. CALLIFER: Leave it to the morning, dear, and then Anne can help you.

John enters in an overcoat, hat in hand.

JOHN: Anne's still not ready. Mother, this is the only children's party I go to these holidays. I'm getting too old for Blind Man's Buff.

MRS. CALLIFER: Well, dear, it was you who insisted.

JOHN (*going to the hall door*): Anne!

MRS. CALLIFER: I don't think she's very fond of Blind Man's Buff either.

JOHN: She has to learn her social obligations. (*Anne enters.*) We are a quarter of an hour late already.

99

ANNE: I know. With any luck we shall miss The Ocean Is Agitated.

MRS. CALLIFER: What's that?

ANNE: It's the most hideous game of the year. Can I have a cocktail, Granny?

MRS. CALLIFER: Of course you can't.

ANNE: He had a whisky. He said he wanted Dutch courage.

JOHN: That's quite different. Come on.

ANNE: We needn't stay long, need we?

MRS. CALLIFER: If you stay as long as your father thinks polite you can have a glass of wine when you come home.

ANNE: Thank you, Granny. Now I can spurn the fruit cup. (*She goes out, followed by John, who makes a despairing gesture.*)

MRS. CALLIFER: How pretty she is.

SARA: Yes, isn't she? (*Busying herself with the holly*): I sometimes wonder what she would have been like if her mother had lived.

MRS. CALLIFER: Do parents influence children? I don't see much of our influence on John.

SARA: Or James?

MRS. CALLIFER (*closing down*): He always went his own road.

SARA: He never spends Christmas here, does he?

MRS. CALLIFER: His work doesn't allow him time.

SARA: Or do you never invite him?

MRS. CALLIFER: It's only because of Anne we celebrate at all. Henry had his own name for the day. He called it Children's Day. He never approved of the word Christmas.

SARA (*ironically*): Why shouldn't we celebrate the great Palestinian religious leader?

MRS. CALLIFER: Oh, you know, dear, Christmas existed long before him.

SARA: Did your husband mind holly?

MRS. CALLIFER: No. That belonged to the ancient pagan festival—so he said. Did you hear a car?

SARA: No.

MRS. CALLIFER: I hope Anne hasn't found some excuse.

SARA: I'll go and see. (*As she crosses the room a bell rings.*)

MRS. CALLIFER: I hate a bell at night.

SARA: Perhaps an extra Christmas mail.

Sara goes out. Mrs. Callifer has her eyes fixed on the door. Who does she expect to see enter? James? William? Certainly she is not expecting Dr. Kreuzer. She doesn't give Sara time to announce him.

MRS. CALLIFER: Dr. Kreuzer!

Pause.

KREUZER: Good evening, Mrs. Callifer.

MRS. CALLIFER: Has something happened to James? Is he with you?

KREUZER: I hoped to find him here.

MRS. CALLIFER: Here? He isn't here. Why didn't you telephone?

KREUZER: Because I have to see you, Mrs. Callifer. If I had telephoned you would have refused to let me come.

MRS. CALLIFER: But what's all the urgency? I don't understand why—

KREUZER: I telephoned to him twice yesterday. He wasn't at home. Again today. Even Mr. Corner didn't know where he was. When you saw him in Nottingham did he talk to you about going away?

MRS. CALLIFER: Perhaps. Vaguely. I can't really remember.

KREUZER: I am very anxious, Mrs. Callifer. You see, I know that he had suicide on his mind.

SARA: Suicide?

KREUZER: He took some pills from my desk. They are quite harmless, but he didn't know that. So you see, I have to know what happened afterwards between the two of you.

MRS. CALLIFER: We talked. What could have happened? We talked of this and that.

102

KREUZER: Did he seem disturbed?

MRS. CALLIFER: I don't know. Perhaps. A little.

SARA: You never told me that.

KREUZER: Mrs. Callifer, I wish you'd be more specific. This is your son.

MRS. CALLIFER: He talked of visiting someone.

KREUZER: Who? (*No answer.*) Who was he going to visit, Mrs. Callifer?

MRS. CALLIFER (*reluctantly*): His uncle.

SARA (*astonished*): William Callifer?

MRS. CALLIFER: It was just a wild notion of his. I don't suppose he went.

KREUZER: Mrs. Callifer, your son is in a very dark place. We in Europe have had experience of dark places. I know a man who lived five days in a sewer without food. The manhole was in the pavement just in front of his home. All day he heard the voices of strangers and at night there were the footsteps of policemen. He stayed there just under the manhole, waiting for his mother to speak to him and tell him it was safe to come out. He couldn't trust even his father.

SARA (*bitterly*): I suppose she never came.

KREUZER: She came.

SARA: Perhaps in Europe they breed mothers.

MRS. CALLIFER (*pleading*): Sara, my dear—

103

SARA: But not here. Oh, no. Not here.

KREUZER: It's time, Mrs. Callifer, to tell us what you know.

MRS. CALLIFER: But there's nothing I *know*.

KREUZER: Your son's in danger. Great danger. Think. If he were hiding in that sewer you'd have risked anything . . .

MRS. CALLIFER: Of course. It would be easy that way. This is different.

SARA: It's no good, Dr. Kreuzer. You're working on a false assumption. Mothers don't necessarily love their children.

MRS. CALLIFER: That's not true, Sara. You know it's not true.

SARA: When I married James I never saw you in our house. But when I divorced him, I became your dear adopted daughter.

MRS. CALLIFER: Henry and I loved you, Sara.

SARA: Yes, so long as James wasn't there. She's upright, Dr. Kreuzer, she's strong, she's loyal, she has all the wifely virtues. But don't look for a mother there.

MRS. CALLIFER: I love him.

SARA: Who? Henry? I don't suppose James told you this, Dr. Kreuzer. It was always Henry—what suited his stomach (not string beans), his mind, his reputation. William Callifer didn't suit it. He had to go. And then her son. If I had a son, I wouldn't sacrifice him for my husband. Why do we have to sacrifice people? Why can't we just let each other be?

MRS. CALLIFER: Henry wasn't selfish, Sara. He was weak, that's all. You don't know yet how weakness can call to you.

SARA: But I don't want to protect anyone—I'm not a god. I'm not strong enough or wise enough and I don't want to be protected either—I'm not that cunning.

MRS. CALLIFER: Haven't you any pity?

SARA: And I haven't that much pride. You don't pity an equal.

KREUZER: Why did he want to see his uncle so suddenly, Mrs. Callifer?

Silence.

SARA: All right. You can sit there and wait for him to die. I can't. Will you drive me to town, Dr. Kreuzer?

KREUZER: If you wish me to.

SARA: I'm going to pack my bags. Someone else will have to decorate—for Children's Day.

Sara leaves. Pause. Then a strained conversation begins.

MRS. CALLIFER: She is very overwrought.

KREUZER: Yes.

MRS. CALLIFER: She won't really go. It's just a mood. I would have been happy to put you up, Dr. Kreuzer.

KREUZER: It's kind of you, but I have to be in London early tomorrow.

Pause.

105

MRS. CALLIFER: Do you think me a monster too?

KREUZER: No. But perhaps I've been treating the wrong patient.

Baston enters.

BASTON: You're Dr. Kreuzer.

MRS. CALLIFER: This is Dr. Baston. (*Baston doesn't shake hands.*)

BASTON (*to Mrs. Callifer*): Sara seems upset. What's this about James attempting suicide again?

KREUZER: Again?

BASTON: When he was fourteen he tried to hang himself.

KREUZER: So that was it?

MRS. CALLIFER: Yes.

KREUZER: And now he knows that?

MRS. CALLIFER: Yes.

KREUZER: I wish I had known of it first. Mrs. Callifer, is that all you have to tell me?

MRS. CALLIFER: Yes.

BASTON: Dr. Kreuzer, this matter of the pills—that's really serious. I think we have to consider whether he wouldn't be better—for a while—in a home. It's hard for you, Mary, but—

MRS. CALLIFER: I've never believed in captivity, even for animals. Don't you remember that letter we all signed?

BASTON: This is different. This is for his good.

MRS. CALLIFER: I've heard people defend zoos that way. The animals are freed from starvation and fear. Oh yes, I know all those answers, Fred. Don't hand them out to me. We fought in the same causes.

BASTON: And sometimes we were wrong. Sometimes we were too general and too emotional. We must avoid sentimentality.

MRS. CALLIFER: That's what we always call a sentiment we don't share, isn't it?

BASTON: We have to deal with facts. At fourteen he tried to kill himself. Since then he's suffered from all kinds of delusions. Melancholia. (*James enters through the open door.*) A sense of persecution. (*Kreuzer and Mrs. Callifer see James. Mrs. Callifer is distressed. She half rises and then sinks down again. Kreuzer leans forward, watching James closely. Baston, his back turned, talking pompously, head lowered, hands behind back, notices nothing.*) You hadn't the chance to observe him, Dr. Kreuzer, when he came here for his father's funeral. I had.

MRS. CALLIFER: Please, Fred.

BASTON: Let me finish, Mary. I admit I have less experience of psychotics than you, Dr. Kreuzer—

JAMES: I'm sorry to interrupt.

BASTON (*quietly*): What on earth—

MRS. CALLIFER: What are you doing here, James?

107

The Potting Shed

JAMES: I've come to see Sara.

MRS. CALLIFER: But it's too late. There's no train.

JAMES: I hitchhiked. Eight hours on the road. It's a beautiful time of year. I like trees bare, so that you can see their shape. I didn't expect to see you, Dr. Kreuzer. I seem to have interrupted a conclave.

BASTON: We were talking of you.

JAMES: I don't suppose you would care for my opinion, but you know I've never felt saner in my life.

BASTON: Trying to kill yourself again—that wasn't exactly sane.

JAMES: Oh, that. That belongs to the past. It won't happen again.

BASTON: I feel strongly that a period of rest—perhaps under Dr. Kreuzer's care—

JAMES: I don't need Dr. Kreuzer's care any longer. You see, the gap's filled. I know what happened.

KREUZER: What do you know?

JAMES: That I killed myself in the potting shed.

BASTON: You see, Dr. Kreuzer?

Even Kreuzer is thrown by James's remark. He gets up, takes a careful look and then moves away. He needs time to digest this new aspect of the case.

BASTON: Did your uncle convince you of this?

JAMES: Oh, no. He believed, like all of you, it was a mistake. It was the only belief he had left. He had given everything to bring me back.

BASTON: The asylums are full of people who think God chose them specially. Dr. Kreuzer, this is a far worse symptom than your stolen pills.

Sara enters in a travelling coat, wearing a scarf.

SARA: James! What are you—

JAMES: I came to see you, Sara.

BASTON: Sara, you'd better know this right away. I want to have James certified.

SARA: Certified? But that's nonsense.

BASTON: He's completely irresponsible.

SARA: But those pills—after all, they weren't dangerous.

BASTON: We are dealing with something worse than pills. James has just told us he killed himself in the potting shed and was—resurrected. By the prayers of his uncle, I suppose.

SARA: James, you never said that. Dr. Baston, you misunderstood.

JAMES: Baston has reported me quite accurately.

SARA: But you are not *mad,* James.

JAMES: That's what they have to decide, isn't it?

BASTON: Well, Dr. Kreuzer, are you satisfied now?

KREUZER: An illusion needn't be dangerous. An illusion can be curative, Dr. Baston.

BASTON: Dr. Kreuzer, how many times do your patients have to attempt suicide before you are ready to certify them?

KREUZER: An attempted suicide is not necessarily serious. Only the suicides that succeed.

BASTON: Not serious. You astonish me, Dr. Kreuzer.

KREUZER: People play-act—to others, to themselves. The majority of attempted suicides never meant to succeed.

BASTON: But sometimes, Dr. Kreuzer, people may succeed through inexperience.

KREUZER: You can hardly gain experience in killing yourself, Dr. Baston.

BASTON: You know very well what I mean. Things may go wrong—a man may stumble on the right number of pills.

KREUZER: Very seldom. We all have great unconscious wisdom.

BASTON: He succeeded the first time.

KREUZER: He what, Dr. Baston?

BASTON (*embarrassed*): I mean he would have succeeded if the gardener had not found him. (*Running hastily on*): You are taking a great responsibility, Dr. Kreuzer, if you don't sign with me. He's your patient. Coroners are apt to take a harsh view of psychiatrists whose patients kill themselves. Has it never happened to you?

KREUZER: Dr. Baston, surely there's another doctor whose opinion we ought to have, if he's alive—the doctor who was here when it happened.

MRS. CALLIFER: Dr. Baston was the doctor.

KREUZER: I see.

BASTON: I can assure you there was nothing—unusual.

KREUZER: You massaged the heart?

BASTON: It was too late.

KREUZER: Too late?

BASTON: He was already conscious when I arrived.

KREUZER: Oh, I see.

BASTON: The layman can't recognize death. He thinks just because a mirror doesn't fog or a leaf on the lips move—

KREUZER: They tried that?

BASTON: If such a test for death was infallible, and it never could be, even then I would not accept a miracle. I would simply say we had to redefine our terms—the concepts, life and death.

MRS. CALLIFER: Henry told himself that too. The trouble was he didn't believe the argument.

BASTON: What on earth are you suggesting, Mary?

MRS. CALLIFER: Henry believed that Potter's story was true. He never spoke of it, but I knew.

111

BASTON: That's nonsense, Mary.

MRS. CALLIFER: Why do you think I was afraid to let James see him when he was dying? Henry could forget so long as he wasn't reminded. If you are guilty, you want to forget. (*To James*): You loved your uncle. You half believed—but your father had a wicked tongue and all the arguments. Oh, it was my fault too. I didn't know how deeply he cut. A child can't stand confusion.

BASTON: Mary, we aren't concerned with trivial mistakes in a child's upbringing. You can't pretend Henry believed that ignorant gardener's story.

MRS. CALLIFER: James, I never wanted to tell you this. I wanted to forget too. Sleeping dogs, Dr. Kreuzer, sleeping dogs. Henry was a fake.

BASTON: You appall me. I always thought you loved him.

MRS. CALLIFER: You know I loved him. One can love a fake. Perhaps it's easier than loving rectitude. All his life he'd written on the necessity for proof. Proof, proof, proof. And then a proof was pushed under his nose, at the bottom of his own garden. Fred, I saw his face. We always knew each other's thoughts. I could hear him saying to himself, "Must I recall all those books and start again?" But I was trained to my job. I began to protect him—my husband, not my son.

BASTON: But *you* didn't believe—

MRS. CALLIFER: No, I didn't. It was a long time before I realized just how much he did.

*In the embarrassed silence a door slams. Voices in the hall.
Anne enters, followed by John.*

ANNE: Hello, Uncle James. Have you come for Christmas?

JOHN: What a gathering!

MRS. CALLIFER: John, take Anne upstairs to bed. We have a
lot to talk about.

ANNE: But you promised me a glass of wine.

MRS. CALLIFER: Tomorrow, Anne. It's late. Now you've had a
nice party—

ANNE: It was the most hideous party of the year.

JOHN: I do wish you'd forget that word "hideous," Anne. You
only picked it up last term. Come along.

JAMES: I'll come up and say good night. I've something for
you.

ANNE: Thank you, Uncle James. I can trust your promises.
(*To Mrs. Callifer*): All right, I'll go. But I've got hideous sus-
picions. (*She is dragged out by John.*)

BASTON: I suppose we must resume—

MRS. CALLIFER: Fred, it's late. Can't we sleep on this?

BASTON: It's gone too far, Mary. We've got to decide— (*James,
reminded by the sight of Anne of his present, draws a toy re-
volver from his pocket, twirling the chamber to see that it's in
working order. Baston becomes rigid. Neither Sara nor*

113

Kreuzer have seen. Mrs. Callifer has, but she recognizes it easily as a toy.) What's that?

JAMES: A gun!

BASTON: I told you he's determined to kill himself.

MRS. CALLIFER: Really, Fred, can't you recognize a toy when you see one?

BASTON (*furious*): Buffoonery!

JAMES: I bought it on the way for Anne. It seemed a suitable present for a detective. I have a magnifying glass here too—but perhaps that's more suitable for Dr. Baston.

SARA: James, you came to see me?

JAMES: Yes.

SARA: Then please, all of you, won't you leave us alone.

BASTON: I won't take the responsibility.

MRS. CALLIFER: Then I will.

SARA: Dr. Kreuzer, my bag's in the hall. I'll be with you in a few minutes.

Mrs. Callifer walks firmly out. Kreuzer follows her. Baston hesitates and then follows too. Pause.

JAMES: Do you think I'm mad?

SARA: I don't know.

JAMES: Is everyone who believes in a God mad?

SARA: Of course not. I suppose I believe in Him—in a way—

on Sundays if the music's good. But James, I'm in such a fog.
I don't know what I think. It would have been such a useless
miracle. It ruined us. It gave you thirty empty years, and your
uncle . . .

JAMES: I don't understand either. But I couldn't believe in a
god so simple I could understand him.

SARA: Why did you come to see me, James?

JAMES: I want you to marry me.

SARA: Sometimes I've dreamed of you saying that. But James,
it didn't work the first time.

JAMES: Can't we try again?

SARA: I remember the same words, but I spoke them.

JAMES: Poetic justice.

SARA: I don't want justice. I love you, but love wasn't enough
before, was it? One's got to understand. When I looked at
you, I used to see nothing. But this belief of yours, James—
it's worse than nothing. It's sent you so far away I can't follow. I can't love a God I don't know exists. I can't pray to a
possibility.

JAMES: I don't even want to pray. Something happened to
me, that's all. Like a street accident. I don't want God. I
don't love God, but He's there—it's no good pretending; He's
in my lungs like air.

SARA: You haven't any proof.

JAMES: Not the kind Baston needs. But don't tell a man who has just seen a ghost he has no proof. I've seen the mark of His footsteps going away.

SARA: Footsteps?

JAMES: Have you ever seen a room from which faith has gone? A room without faith—oh, that can be pretty and full of flowers. You can fill it up with Regency furniture and the best modern pictures, but a room from which faith has gone is quite different. Like a marriage from which love has gone. All that's left are habits and pet names and sentimental objects picked up on beaches and in foreign towns that don't mean anything any more. And patience, patience everywhere like a fog.

SARA: Like our marriage?

JAMES: No. We were like the room without faith. We hadn't lost anything valuable.

SARA: Don't be cruel, James. Not tonight.

JAMES: I didn't mean to be. I'd no idea what love was in those days. I was the wrong man to make a deathbed marriage. Nothing mattered. If I slept with you, what did it matter? We were all going to be as dead as last year's dog. Now, when I look at you, I see someone who will never die forever. (*Pause. She makes no response.*) Sara, you never believed I wanted you and you were right. Your kiss was always a question, and I hadn't got an answer. I couldn't love you any more than you can love a tree, a glass of wine, a cat.

SARA: People love cats.

JAMES: Then they don't know the meaning of the word.

SARA: But James, I wasn't kissing anyone immortal when I was kissing you. There were no cosmic messages. I was only saying, "I have remembered to order the steaks. And I'll be here tonight and tomorrow night and the night after." I don't want eternity, James. I'm bored with eternity, going on and on like a long litany on a wet day.

JAMES: It's time that bores us, interminable time. I move my hand. It moves in space and time. When there's no time there'll be no movement any more. When we think, we think one thing after another. Time, again. When there's no time we shan't think any more.

SARA: A frightening world.

JAMES: I've been there and I'm not frightened.

SARA: But time is all I know.

JAMES: Oh, I love time too. I'm not impatient for eternity. It's the same as when you love a woman. If you are going to see her in a few hours, you love the hours. They have *her* importance.

SARA: Darling, please try to understand. Even if there was a miracle, I want to forget it.

JAMES: Like my father?

SARA: Not like your father. I love you. But I hate big things— Everest and the Empire State Building. I don't want to be

117

important. I don't like important people. They're—anti-aphrodisiac to me.

JAMES: Everest exists.

SARA: I wish you'd brought something back to prove it, then. Like the lover in the story—one out-of-season flower. Dear, I'm scared. Suppose—

JAMES: Yes?

SARA: Suppose this time I failed you. No, don't speak. You've got to understand me. I don't want to lose you again, but I'd rather lose you than fail you—and if you're looking for someone important, I won't come up to the specifications, that's all.

JAMES: Sara—

SARA: We don't have to convince each other. I don't want to share a faith—only understand. Give me a little time. Time to think. (*She goes toward the door.*)

JAMES: Don't go away.

SARA: It would be no good going away. I'm no good at thinking alone.

Mrs. Callifer enters.

MRS. CALLIFER: Oh, I didn't know you two—

SARA: I'm just going.

MRS. CALLIFER: Not to London, Sara?

SARA: Just to bed. I'm sorry about what I said to you.

MRS. CALLIFER: Home truths are good sometimes.

SARA: I was so smug, wasn't I, condemning you? At least you were trying to protect someone you loved. And here I am, just trying to protect myself. Good night, Mother. Good night, James.

JAMES: I'll see you tomorrow.

SARA: Of course. (*She goes.*)

JAMES: I'm sorry, Mother, too. A miracle in a family must be worse than a murder case.

MRS. CALLIFER: It's a cruel God you believe in.

JAMES: Perhaps He had no choice.

MRS. CALLIFER: A God who can't choose?

JAMES: God is conditioned, isn't He? If He's all-powerful, He can't weaken. If He knows everything, He can't forget. If He's love, He can't hate. Perhaps if someone asks with enough love, He has to give.

MRS. CALLIFER: People are asking all the time.

JAMES: Are they? It needs a lot of belief and a lot of love.

MRS. CALLIFER: But your uncle doesn't believe.

JAMES: Oh, yes, he does. I left him praying.

Pause.

MRS. CALLIFER: Give us time, James. You mustn't mind the fuss we've made. You've spoilt our certainties.

119

JAMES: I didn't mean to.

MRS. CALLIFER: It seems such an enormous supernatural act. But then our certainties—they were pretty big too. It was all right to doubt the existence of God as your grandfather did in the time of Darwin. Doubt—that was human liberty. But my generation, we didn't doubt, we *knew*. I don't believe in this miracle—but I'm not sure any longer. We are none of us sure. When you aren't sure, you are alive. What will you do, James?

JAMES: Marry Sara, I hope.

MRS. CALLIFER: That's a very simple aim.

JAMES: I've lived with the complex long enough.

MRS. CALLIFER: When I look at you I don't see a madman or a miracle.

JAMES: No?

MRS. CALLIFER: I see all those years when you were happy. Days at the seaside. Parties at Christmas. All the ordinary life we had before it happened.

JAMES: And the toy spade?

MRS. CALLIFER: How you loved that spade. You'd kept it all those years. Potter found it under you, as though you'd taken it in your hand when you climbed on that chair.

JAMES: Can I stay here awhile, Mother, and cease to be a stranger?

MRS. CALLIFER: I've had your room prepared. I hope they've given you enough blankets. But if you're cold knock on the wall. I shall hear. Go to bed now.

JAMES: Will Anne be asleep?

MRS. CALLIFER: I doubt it.

JAMES: I just wanted to give her this. Good night, Mother.

MRS. CALLIFER: Good night. James.

He passes Dr. Kreuzer in the doorway.

JAMES: Good night, Dr. Kreuzer.

KREUZER: I'm just leaving. Good-bye, Callifer.

JAMES: We'll be seeing each other soon? Nottingham or elsewhere?

KREUZER: I don't give up a friend any more than a patient.

James leaves.

KREUZER: Is your daughter ready?

MRS. CALLIFER: Sara won't be leaving with you, Dr. Kreuzer.

KREUZER: I'm glad. Just now, waiting for her in the dining room, I heard you come in from outside?

MRS. CALLIFER: I've been in the garden.

KREUZER: Wasn't it cold?

MRS. CALLIFER: I went down to the potting shed. And suddenly I wasn't frightened. There was nothing ghostly there. The ground wasn't holy. There were no voices and whispers and messages. Only the boxes of seeds and the gardening tools, and I thought perhaps even miracles are ordinary. There was a girl in the village once they thought had died— do you think perhaps things like that are happening all the time everywhere?

KREUZER: I don't know. I don't much mind one way or the other.

MRS. CALLIFER: I thought you wanted the truth. You are a scientist.

KREUZER: I only want a relative truth to make life tolerable.

MRS. CALLIFER: That's not very brave, is it?

KREUZER: Courage can be a very difficult neurosis.

James enters.

JAMES: Anne isn't in her room.

MRS. CALLIFER: Perhaps the bathroom.

JAMES: I've looked everywhere upstairs.

MRS. CALLIFER: The pantry.

JAMES: It was the first place I thought of.

He is looking at the curtains of the window seat. He draws back the curtains. In the window seat Anne lies asleep with the window open behind her.

MRS. CALLIFER: She must have got through the window. The detective asleep at her post.

ANNE (*stretching and yawning*): Oh, I've had such a funny dream. I was going down the path to the potting shed, and there was an enormous lion there fast asleep.

JAMES: What did you do?

ANNE: I woke it up.

MRS. CALLIFER: Did it eat you?

ANNE: No, it only licked my hand.

CURTAIN